Cantigas

The Lockert Library of Poetry in Translation

SERIES EDITORS
Peter Cole, Richard Sieburth, and Rosanna Warren

SERIES EDITOR EMERITUS (1991–2016)
Richard Howard

For other titles in the Lockert Library, see the list at the end of this volume.

Cantigas

Galician-Portuguese Troubadour Poems

Translated by
Richard Zenith

Princeton University Press
Princeton and Oxford

Published by Princeton University Press
41 William Street, Princeton, New Jersey 08540
6 Oxford Street, Woodstock, Oxfordshire OX20 1TR

press.princeton.edu

All Rights Reserved

Library of Congress Cataloging-in-Publication Data
Names: Zenith, Richard, translator, writer of introduction.
Title: Cantigas : Galician-Portuguese troubadour poems / translated and introduced by Richard Zenith.
Description: Princeton : Princeton University Press, 2022. | Series: The Lockert Library of poetry in translation | Includes bibliographical references.
Identifiers: LCCN 2021035939 (print) | LCCN 2021035940 (ebook) | ISBN 9780691179407 (paperback ; acid-free paper) | ISBN 9780691179391 (hardback ; acid-free paper) | ISBN 9780691207414 (ebook)
Subjects: LCSH: Portuguese poetry—To 1500—Translations into English. | Songs, Portuguese—Texts. | Troubadour songs—Texts. | LCGFT: Poetry.
Classification: LCC PQ9163.E6 C36 2022 (print) | LCC PQ9163.E6 (ebook) | DDC 869.1/0408—dc23
LC record available at https://lccn.loc.gov/2021035939
LC ebook record available at https://lccn.loc.gov/2021035940

British Library Cataloging-in-Publication Data is available

Editorial: Anne Savarese and James Collier
Production Editorial: Ellen Foos and Jaden Young
Text and Jacket/Cover Design: Pamela L. Schnitter
Production: Erin Suydam
Publicity: Jodi Price and Carmen Jimenez
Copyeditor: Kathleen Kageff

Cover art: (*right*) Wave pattern by Twins Design Studio / Shutterstock; (*middle left*) Cantiga de Santa Maria, no. 340. Album / Alamy Stock Photo. (*bottom left*) Cantiga de Santa Maria, no. 95, F137. Album / Alamy Stock Photo

The Lockert Library of Poetry in Translation is supported by a bequest from Charles Lacy Lockert

This book has been composed in Adobe Text Pro

Printed on acid-free paper. ∞

Printed in the United States of America

10 9 8 7 6 5 4 3 2 1

CONTENTS

Cantigas

INTRODUCTION

One Saturday afternoon in the mid-1980s I was browsing the stacks of the Georgetown University Library, trying to educate myself in the varieties of poetry written in Portuguese. After graduating from college, I had spent three years in Brazil, where I learned the Portuguese language and began translating a couple of contemporary Brazilian poets, but I was largely ignorant of the tradition behind those poets. Where to begin? I picked out two or three books at random before spotting, on a higher shelf, several tall tomes with *Cancioneiro* printed on the spines. Pulling them down and gazing at the pages, I unexpectedly entered a literary realm whose existence I'd never heard of: troubadour songs—*cantigas*—in Galician-Portuguese.

I was familiar with Ezra Pound's translations of poems by Arnaut Daniel, Bertran de Born, and other troubadours from Provence, and I had recently bought a copy of Paul Blackburn's splendid *Proensa: An Anthology of Troubadour Poetry*, but while I could certainly sense affinities between the troubadour tradition I already knew and the one I was just now discovering, it was the differences that were striking. One of them had to do with the settings. Not until the fifteenth century would Portuguese and Spanish navigators initiate the so-called Age of Discoveries, but I soon realized that in some of the cantigas from the 1200s the ocean was already an almost mythical and at times poetically hypnotic presence, variously suggestive of risk, possibility, and tragedy. Paio Gomes Charinho, a troubadour who spent time at sea as a naval officer, compared its devastating power to that of love:

1

Those who spend their lives at sea
think there is no pain in the world
as great as their pain, and no fate worse
than a seaman's fate, but consider me:
    the pain of love made me forget
    the pain of the sea, so harsh and yet

as nothing next to that greatest pain,
the pain of love that God ordains.

And the cantiga continues, its haunting lament growing in intensity.

Another sea-inspired cantiga I noticed in my early forays is by one Meendinho, about whom nothing at all is known. His only surviving cantiga had nevertheless earned him a rank of honor among the approximately 150 Galician-Portuguese troubadours. This cantiga, unusually dramatic, belongs to a female-voiced genre peculiar to Iberia. Danger is announced at the outset:

Sitting in the chapel of San Simón,
soon I was surrounded by the rising ocean,
    waiting for my lover, still waiting.

Before the altar of the chapel, waiting,
soon I was surrounded by the ocean's waves,
    waiting for my lover, still waiting.

While the speaker faithfully waits, the waters keep rising until, at the end of the cantiga, we can almost envision her being engulfed:

Without a boatman, unused to rowing,
I'll die, a fair girl, in the heaving ocean,
    waiting for my lover, still waiting.

Without a boatman to row me away,
I'll die, a fair girl, in the ocean's waves,
    waiting for my lover, still waiting.

Yet another distinctive feature of Galician-Portuguese po-
etry—well illustrated by the Meendinho cantiga—is the use
of repetition with small displacements and variations. There
was a time not long before my discovery of the cantigas that
I listened obsessively to an early composition by Philip
Glass, *Music with Changing Parts*, and cantigas like Meend-
inho's enchanted me for being similarly minimalistic. We
might call them "poetry with changing parts."

Lured in by the cited poems and others like these, as well
as by poems very different from these—there are hundreds
of satiric, sometimes quite bawdy cantigas—I decided to
translate a selection of them into English, a task that quickly
proved to be far more challenging than anticipated. When
translating any poem, one must first identify where the po-
etry *is*. What makes it a valid, successful poem? In the can-
tigas, whose narrative and ideational content is rather slight,
the poetry clearly resides in their formal aspects—meter,
rhyme, musical repetitions, and so forth. Paul Blackburn did
a marvelous job of conveying the spirit of the Provençal
troubadours he translated by using a poetic-musical idiom
of the twentieth century. In the case of the cantigas, many
of which are genuinely naïve, I doubted that this method
would yield similarly admirable results. It has so far proven
impossible to convincingly replicate, in English, the com-
plex rhyme schemes (not to mention other poetic complexi-
ties) of William of Aquitaine, Arnaut Daniel, Marcabru, and
their peers, but to attempt something of the sort seemed to
me the only viable path for translating the cantigas. Unlike
with Provençal poetry, the simpler verse patterns and me-
lodic grammar of the cantigas allow at least the possibility
of their being successfully simulated. I strove to preserve
those patterns and that grammar.

The proverbial advantage of leaving one's poems in a
drawer for many years and then returning to them as a cold,
objective reader also holds true for translations of poetry. In
1995 I published, in England, a bilingual selection titled *113
Galician-Portuguese Troubadour Poems*, which has long

been out of print. Revisited by me twenty-five years later, not one of those translations has remained intact, and some have been drastically refashioned. I have also added eleven new cantigas to the mix. In these intervening years I have translated many other poets, from recent and not so recent centuries, but I still find that the cantigas require more technical and creative sweat—along with patient waiting for the serendipitous workings of chance—than any other poetry I've rendered into English. The greatest difficulty? To make them simply sing.

◆ ◆ ◆

"Galician-Portuguese" is a modern coinage for the Romance language spoken in northwestern Iberia in the early Middle Ages. It is the ancestor of Galician and Portuguese, two distinct but closely related languages. As the Kingdom of Galicia (situated north of Portugal) was brought more firmly under the control of the Kingdom of Castile, especially from the fifteenth century on, Castilian Spanish supplanted the local language in official documents and other forms of writing. Even as a spoken language, Galician slowly lost ground to Spanish, especially in the large towns. During the nineteenth-century Rexurdimento (Renaissance), writers such as the poet Rosalía de Castro reasserted Galician as a written language, and although the Franco regime actively suppressed it in the twentieth century, Galician nowadays boasts a thriving literature. Portuguese has had a happier destiny, spreading southward in the peninsula as the Kingdom of Portugal pushed southward, and then to Africa, Brazil, and a few pockets in Asia. Today it is the world's seventh most spoken language.

Snatches of Galician-Portuguese appear in Latin administrative documents going back to the ninth century, but the earliest known texts written wholly in Galician-Portuguese are the cantigas of Iberian troubadours, active between the end of the twelfth and the middle of the fourteenth centuries. By then the separate national identities of Galicia and

4

Portugal were well established, and their languages began to diverge. So when we speak of Galician-Portuguese literature, we mean the sung poems called cantigas and nothing else.

Much of this literature, oddly enough, was written not in Galicia or Portugal but in the Spanish kingdoms of León and Castile—a fact eloquently demonstrated by the example of King Alfonso X, who became the ruler of both kingdoms in 1252. Known as "el Sabio," the Learned, because of his fervent intellectual activity, Alfonso X oversaw numerous translations of scholarly Arabic and Hebrew works into Castilian and produced major treatises on astronomy and history, likewise in Castilian, but he wrote all his large output of poetry in Galician-Portuguese. To understand why, we need to back up a little in time.

Troubadours from Occitania[1]—the area of southern France where the poetry of *fin'amor*, "refined love," originated in the late eleventh century—traveled in all directions during the twelfth century. With the onset of the Albigensian Crusade (1209–29), which saw Catholic zealots and French armies ravage Occitania to stamp out the heresy of the allegedly Gnostic Cathars, the troubadours would go abroad in even greater numbers than before. As early as the mid-1100s their influence had given rise to the trouvères of northern France while profoundly affecting the style of the Minnesänger in Germany. A few decades later troubadour movements sprang up in Italy and Catalonia, where the locals composed songs not in their native tongues but in Occitan.[2] In western Iberia, Peire Vidal and other troubadours arriving from beyond the Pyrenees naturally visited Santiago de Compostela, the capital of Galicia and the most

[1] The words *Provence* and *Provençal* have been used inexactly since medieval times to indicate the whole of southern France and the language that was spoken there. Nowadays the geographically and linguistically more accurate terms *Occitania* and *Occitan* are preferred.
[2] Occitan poetry would also inspire the Sicilian school, which flourished a little later and produced the first lyric poetry in an Italian vernacular.

5

popular pilgrimage site after Rome, but for financial patronage they tended to gravitate around the powerful royal courts of León and Castile rather than the poorer courts of Galicia and Portugal. It was nevertheless in these latter kingdoms, as the twelfth century turned into the thirteenth, that the new poetry found especially fertile terrain. Exactly how it happened remains a mystery, but a new court poetry—modeled after Occitan poetry but with some strikingly different features—emerged in the Galician-Portuguese language, which became the poetic *koiné* for much of Christian Iberia.

Although their cantigas have disappeared, we know there were early Galician troubadours who sojourned in Catalonia (where a tradition of *langue d'oc*[3] poetry had already taken hold) in the late twelfth century. The oldest surviving cantiga in Galician-Portuguese, probably written in 1196, was by a Portuguese nobleman, Joam Soares de Paiva, who was living at the time in Castile or Aragon. Perhaps he came into contact with some of the Occitan troubadours residing in those kingdoms, learned their poetic art, translated it into his own language, and took it back to Portugal. Equally revealing—for the story of how the cantigas might have evolved—is the case of Garcia Mendes de Eixo, a Portuguese nobleman who wrote a troubadour song in the langue d'oc during a period of exile in León, around 1215, and whose offspring included two troubadours, Gonçalo Garcia de Sousa and Fernão Garcia Esgaravunha, both of whom wrote their songs in Galician-Portuguese. As these examples show, the first seeds of Galician-Portuguese troubadour poetry came from abroad. But they did not really flower until the 1220s, when more than twenty poets of the new style were active in the courts of Galician and Portuguese noblemen. In the mid-1200s this poetic movement attained its full splendor, at the royal courts of Afonso III

---

[3] "Òc" is the Occitan word for "yes."

(reigned 1248–79) in Portugal and especially Alfonso X (reigned 1252–84) in Castile.

The civil war in Portugal that led to Afonso III's accession, together with the military campaigns to reconquer southern Iberia from the Moors, caused a number of Portuguese troubadours to relocate to Castile, where many of them eventually ended up at the cosmopolitan court of Alfonso X, a proverbially generous patron. Troubadours from all over—Castile, León, Galicia, Portugal, and Occitania—flocked around the king, who seems to have been infatuated not only with their poetry but also with Galician-Portuguese, the language used for most of their compositions, though the transplanted Occitans continued to write in their own language. The king himself composed at least forty-four, mostly satiric troubadour songs, and he oversaw the composition of more than four hundred *cantigas de Santa Maria* (songs in praise of Holy Mary). A few years earlier Gonzalo de Berceo, a cleric from northern Spain, had written a collection of verses praising Mary in Castilian (*Milagros de Nuestra Señora*), but Alfonso's Marian songs, like his secular songs, were all written in Galician-Portuguese.

Alfonso's attachment to this language may be partly explained by the fact that he spent part of his childhood in Galicia, but he had another reason for appreciating this foreign idiom: it accentuated the artificiality of a literature into which the few, not the many, were initiated. The main audience for troubadour poetry consisted of other troubadours and the members of the courts that protected them. They were privy to the conventions that regulated the poetic discourse, particularly when love was the theme. In their love songs the Galician-Portuguese troubadours—like the Occitan poets they emulated—endowed certain words with special meanings. Thus *coita*, meaning "suffering," referred specifically to the painful anxiety felt by someone in love. And *ben*, meaning "goodness" or "benefit," served as a code word for the favor that a beloved might (or might not) show the lover.

◆ ◆ ◆

Some say that the Occitan troubadours actually invented romantic love, with their poetry being both an idealization of this feeling and a projection of it. These poet-composers transferred the feudal concept of vassalage as well as the Christian idealization of Mary to the lover's relationship with his lady: he owes her his "service" as if she were his lord, and he adores her from a distance as one would the immaculate and inaccessible Virgin Mary. Certain of the troubadours were no doubt very much in love with their ladies, others less so, and in some cases their love was pure fiction. Joam Baveca, a Galician troubadour in Alfonso X's court, complained in one of his cantigas about certain colleagues who "do wrong to us who truly love" by swearing a love that's "merely feigned," so that "the ladies think we're lying too." But whether or not they were sincerely loved, the flesh-and-blood ladies of the court were virtually unrecognizable under the generic, model lady that was projected onto them and then venerated in song. The troubadours were thus able to have love—in what they claimed was its most elevated form—quite independently of there being a willing woman, and any lady would do, even one (indeed, *especially* one) who completely ignored him, impossible loves being the more noble and worthwhile.

Besides the love songs known as *cansos*, the Occitan poets also composed *sirventes*, which commented on society, on political situations, or on specific individuals, sometimes through satire. The Galician-Portuguese poets took the satiric mode to the heights, or depths, of malice and indecency. This was nowhere truer than in Alfonso X's court, where the troubadours poked fun at religious and political figures, chickenhearted soldiers, and promiscuous women, to name a few of the favorite targets. And they especially liked to cavil among themselves via dialogued cantigas known in Occitan as *tensons—tenções* in Galician-Portuguese. In the world of their cantigas the troubadours could live great loves with aristocratic detachment and fight duels with words instead of swords.

The possibility of remaking the world must have been a great comfort to Alfonso X, many of whose real-life battles foundered. Although he succeeded in affirming Castile as the most powerful kingdom of Iberia, he failed in his bid to be elected Holy Roman emperor, had mixed results trying to suppress insurgent Moors and nobles, and was abandoned by his subjects when his own son rose up against him. It was an agitated reign. But in the literary realm the king could take satisfaction or at least some consolation, offsetting his defeats with the victory of well-rendered poetry, of which his "Song of a Man Weary of Scorpions" is an illuminating example. The narrator of this cantiga expresses utter disillusion with his life as a knight in arms, and he dreams of leading a simpler existence, selling oil and flour from a small boat that would ply up and down the coast. Though Alfonso's outward circumstances had nothing in common with those of the disillusioned knight (described as a sentinel who made rounds), and though it would be absurd to suppose that he entertained notions of laying aside his crown to become a flour merchant, the poem seems to be obliquely autobiographical, linked to its author's weariness at having to fight battles, crush revolts, and deal with a bitterly divided family. Some critics have suggested that this cantiga, written in the first person, has no connection at all with the king's personal life but parodies, rather, a timorous soldier afraid to take up arms and go into battle. If they are right, then Alfonso's ability to assume such a starkly different poetic persona stands out as an even more remarkable feat. Either way, poetry had asserted itself as another plane of reality—conditioned by religion and feudal society but autonomous, transforming, and in a certain way untouchable. The troubadour poetry that developed in Occitania and spread around other parts of Europe was one of the first expressions of the revolutionary individualism that was to shake the church's foundations through heterodox reform movements and eventually lead to the Renaissance.

After the death of Alfonso X, in 1284, some of the troubadours of his entourage transferred to the court of King Dinis of Portugal, who had ascended the throne in 1279. The most prolific of all the troubadours, Dinis, like the king of Castile, led a double life in his cantigas, using them to reshape his experience but also, and above all, to afford himself the ennobling, exalting experience of poetry. King Dinis had a long and highly successful, mostly peaceful reign, lasting until 1325, but Galician-Portuguese troubadour poetry was now in decline. With the arrival of the Black Death, in 1348, the age of the troubadours came to an end on the peninsula as in the rest of Europe.

◆ ◆ ◆

One of King Dinis's sons, Pedro Afonso, Count of Barcelos (ca. 1285–54), was among the last of the Galician-Portuguese troubadours. He was also responsible for compiling the massive *Livro das cantigas*, which built on a previous compilation, enlarged with more recently composed cantigas. Neither that original compilation nor *Livro das cantigas* has survived, but copies made from them and known as *cancioneiros*—songbooks—have preserved for us some 1,680 cantigas (not counting King Alfonso's *Songs in Praise of Holy Mary*). Almost all the music for these songs has unfortunately been lost.

Scanning the cancioneiros, even without reading or understanding a word, one can notice repeating shapes and patterns. The cantigas are almost all short but not too: three or four stanzas of from three to seven lines is the general rule. A majority of cantigas have refrains, apparently a legacy from the native song tradition. The texts without refrains are known as cantigas of *meestria* (mastery), because they require greater thematic development and technical skill, although they never attain the complexity of the Occitan songs that were their precursors. The cantigas with refrains more often than not have six lines with three rhymes following an *abbaCC* pattern or, occasionally, an *ababCC* pattern, in which *CC* is the refrain. The songs of meestria usually have seven lines with three rhymes following one of various patterns, *abbacca* being the most frequent. Some of the cantigas have a closing couplet or triple known as a *fiinda*. Corresponding to the Occitan *tornada*, or the French envoi, it serves to conclude the argument of the cantiga, sometimes in the form of a punch line. In rare cases, the fiinda may have more or fewer than the customary two or three lines, and some cantigas have more than one fiinda.

Poor in strophic variety, the cantigas also present a reduced number of metrical schemes. And while the Galician-Portuguese poets occasionally succeeded in keeping the same rhymes from stanza to stanza (as in nos. 113 and 114), usually they preserved only the pattern. But if in some respects the Galician-Portuguese school seems a dim reflection of Occitan virtuosity, it shimmers thanks to its fascinating, original use of parallelism, a technique evident in the Meendinho cantiga discussed above. Loosely definable as "repetition with a difference," parallelism takes several forms, the most poetically effective being the literal or linguistic kind, based on the principle of *leixa-pren* (let go–take up). Typically found in cantigas with refrains, it is beautifully exemplified in cantiga 77, by Pero Meogo:

> Levou-s'aa alva, levou-s'a velida,
> vai lavar cabelos na fontana fria;
> leda dos amores, dos amores leda.

> Levou-s'aa alva, levou-s'a louçana,
> vai lavar cabelos na fria fontana;
> leda dos amores, dos amores leda.

> Vai lavar cabelos na fontana fria,
> passou seu amigo, que lhi ben queria;
> leda dos amores, dos amores leda.

Vai lavar cabelos na fria fontana:
passa seu amigo, que a muit'amava;
leda dos amores, dos amores leda.

Passa seu amigo, que lhi ben queria,
o cervo do monte a áugua volvia;
leda dos amores, dos amores leda.

Passa seu amigo, que a muit'amava:
o cervo do monte volvia a áugua;
leda dos amores, dos amores leda.

Stanzas 2, 4, and 6 repeat the information presented in stanzas 1, 3, and 5, but with slight variations, certain end words being substituted by synonyms: *velida* (fair) → *louçana* (pretty), *queria* (liked) → *amava* (loved). At other times, the last two words of the line change position: *fontana fria* → *fria fontana* (cold spring), *a áugua volvia* → *volvia a áugua* (stirred up the water). At first glance the even-numbered stanzas might appear identical to the odd ones preceding them, but the lines are never exactly the same. On the other hand, a line from each stanza is repeated verbatim two stanzas down, but with a displacement: the second lines of the first two stanzas become the first lines of stanzas 3 and 4, whose second lines in turn become the first lines of stanzas 5 and 6. The verbal house of mirrors is topped off by a refrain in which *leda dos amores* (happy with love) reechoes in inverse form as *dos amores leda*.

The ensemble of these poetic restatements has a mesmerizing effect, heightening the listener's (and nowadays the reader's) sense of the girl's rapture and innocence. It's as if the simple meeting of a girl with her lover were taking place on an otherworldly plane. This may seem an overstatement, but less so when we consider that the water, hair, and mountain stag—elements that recur in other cantigas—are charged with symbolic meaning.

Semantic parallelism, which is the repetition not of words but of ideas or subject matter, is well illustrated by cantigas 6 and 81. In these songs there is little or no narrative progress; the first stanza contains the whole story, and successive stanzas merely repeat the information in other words. While this kind of parallelism can dramatize the gravity of a particular feeling or predicament, it risks monotony.

A fragmentary treatise on the troubadours' art, found in the largest of the surviving cancioneiros, describes other poetic devices, which I explain in the notes to cantigas where they occur: cantiga 90 for a characteristic usage of enjambment (*atá fiinda*), cantiga 75 for the "missing rhyme" (*palavra perduda*), cantiga 82 for word doubling (*dobre*), and cantiga 16 for modified word doubling (*mozdobre*). The poetic treatise also describes (though part of this description has been lost) the three major types of secular troubadour songs: *cantigas de amor, cantigas de amigo,* and *cantigas de escárnio e maldizer.*

◆ ◆ ◆

The cantiga de amor, which derived directly from the Occitan canso, dominated the output of the first Galician-Portuguese troubadours and enjoyed, in the courtly circuit, more prestige than other cantiga varieties. Scholars, however, have often passed harsh judgment on the cantigas de amor. "Tremendously monotonous, sterile and conventional in their ideas, expressions and metrical forms" is how they were characterized by Carolina Michaëlis de Vasconcelos (1851–1925) in her critical edition of the Ajuda Palace songbook, the oldest of the surviving cancioneiros.[4] She had a point, but if we selectively pass over about half of the seven hundred or so cantigas de amor that have come down to us, we are left with a body of poetry that presents considerable interest and variety.

[4] Vasconcelos, *Cancioneiro da Ajuda*, 2:598.

13

The institution of feudalism arrived later and less decisively in western Iberia. It did not use feudal terminology in a systematic way, and while relations of vassalage were common enough, the associated rituals of homage (*immixtio manuum*, the oath of fidelity, the formal kiss) were less prevalent, less important. Knowing but a pale version of the feudal relation of lord and vassal, the Galician-Portuguese troubadours could produce no better than a pale version of the canso that was founded on that relation. They addressed the lady of their cantigas de amor as *senhor* (later feminized to become the modern *senhora* of Portuguese and *señora* of Spanish), but they didn't have a clear idea of the homage they owed this "lord" or of the benefit she owed him, her "vassal." The Occitan troubadour compared the beauty of his lady (*midons*) to nature's most splendid phenomena, and he invested her with the qualities of a powerful and life-giving lord; the peninsular poet merely accentuated his *senhor(a)*'s ladylike virtues, piling on limp adjectives like "fair," "sensible," and "worthy." Bernart de Ventadorn and his Occitan peers are condemned to frustration because the object of their love is a perfect ideal that would, if she yielded, become less than perfect, but they can at least delight in their praise of that perfection and can realize love on paper, as it were; the Galician-Portuguese poet rarely achieves such a sublime projection, so that his focus turns back on himself ("Poor me!"), and his rejected love knows no transcendence.

Courtly love becomes the occasion for an obsessive sadness in the Galician-Portuguese domain. The playful and exultant spirit of langue d'oc poetry—its *joi!*—gives way to a self-pitying litany of love's depressing effects. The poet loses sleep, goes insane, or (and this is the all-too-common trope) dies on account of his love. But he takes pride, at least, in his suffering. While admitting that the Occitan poets were incomparable versifiers, King Dinis held up his greater inner torment as proof that his love was more sincere (no. 114). If

14

"sincere love" implies self-absorption in one's own feeling, that might explain some of the infelicitous poetry found in the cantigas de amor. But King Dinis did prove himself capable of focusing all his attention on the lady, in a panegyric he significantly described as a song "in Provençal style" (no. 113). A few other Galician-Portuguese troubadours managed to describe their ladies in original, concrete language, and Joam Garcia de Guilhade left us a unique love song about a green-eyed lady (no. 21). This same Garcia de Guilhade, refreshingly ironic and a disdainer of clichés, composed a nonconforming cantiga de amor in which (no. 26), after recalling all the men whose unrequited love makes them want to die, he exclaims:

> But, my lady, while I may see you,
> I'll always want to live
> and keep on waiting!

And there is nothing sad about Airas Nunes, who in the fourteen lines of cantiga 88 celebrates his love with a euphoric array of images from nature, which he hails as the inspiration for creating his songs.

The Galician-Portuguese troubadours, in any case, had good reasons for feeling glum, since for many of them a female partner was a practical impossibility. Because feudalism arrived late, it was only in the thirteenth century that the Portuguese aristocracy began to regulate the division of family wealth—or rather, its nondivision. *Morgadios* (akin to French *majorats* and English fee tails) assured that virtually all property would be inherited by the eldest son, so as to prevent the piecemeal breakup of landed estates and the scattering of family fortunes, along with family prestige. Younger sons were given supporting roles but expected to remain celibate. Aristocratic young ladies, meanwhile, were reserved for strategic marriages or else shuttled off to a convent. No wonder we find so many troubadours—a majority

15

of whom were noblemen, and very often amorously frustrated noblemen—obsessed with actual or hypothetical ladies forever out of their reach.

Whether they were forcibly celibate, forced into a marriage for the sake of a family alliance, or simply unlucky in love, the Galician-Portuguese troubadours could get their revenge through the cantigas de amigo, which are in some ways the exact inverse of the cantigas de amor. Adopting the female point of view, the cantiga de amigo is usually narrated by an unmarried girl or young woman who pines after her boyfriend, sometimes addressing him directly, or else comments on their relationship and on the hopes, anxieties, or disillusions it arouses. The coita, or suffering, endured by the man in the cantigas de amor now becomes the woman's experience—if her beloved is far away. If, on the other hand, he's close by, the relationship can be pleasurable for both him and her. She might at times resist the advances of her amigo, but on the whole she's complicit. She meets with him at appointed times and places, and in some songs it's obvious that the two sweethearts do much more than chat and make eyes at each other—which is never the case in the cantigas de amor. In a cantiga de amigo by Joam Guilhade, the woman apparently breaks up with him precisely because he didn't make any advances; she's weary of keeping up their merely platonic relationship (no. 27).

Female-voiced songs written by men were not unique to the Iberian Peninsula. A few trouvères wrote *chansons de femme*, and the Minnesänger composed *Mädchenlieder*, but the voluminous output and distinctive character of the approximately five hundred cantigas de amigo have no parallel in other song traditions. That in itself suggests that they must have partly derived from a local, presumably oral tradition. Despite being integrated into a courtly poetry inspired by the Occitan troubadours, the cantigas de amigo, with rare exceptions, kept the refrain that is typical of folk music, and some of them mention dancing. It was the cantigas de amigo that brought parallelism into Galician-Portuguese poetry, and the leixa-pren technique—whereby a stanza takes up a line from the preceding stanza before moving the ball forward—betokens a primitive, responsorial type of singing, with the repeated lines serving as an aid to memory. While the technically rigorous poems of Occitania almost never admitted a less than perfect rhyme, and the cantigas de amor only rarely did, the cantigas de amigo frequently resorted to assonant rhyme. In the Pero Meogo cantiga quoted above, we find *velida* rhyming with *fria, fontana* with *amava*, and *amava* with *áugua*.

The cantigas de amigo are in a certain way ritualistic, presenting concise moments of intense drama on an open stage: the outdoor world common to all. The woods, streams, lakes, and meadows, and especially the seaside are typical places where the girl longs or waits for her beloved, or actually meets him. Sometimes the setting is a local shrine in Galicia or Portugal—visited not for spiritually edifying purposes but to facilitate amorous encounters. In cantiga 84 a girl incites other girls to visit a small-town shrine so that they can dance for their gawking boyfriends while their mothers, inside the church, "light candles for our souls and theirs." It's not clear, in this case, whether the mothers know what their enamored daughters are up to. In some cantigas the mother is an enabler of her daughter's passion; in others she advises caution; in cantiga 76 she displays an attitude of practical resignation. Not only the mother but also the girl's female friends (sometimes called "sisters") frequently appear in the cantigas de amigo, which are often dialogued.

The likelihood of an ancient female song tradition on the peninsula finds support in the *kharja* (exit), which was the final segment of the *muwashshah*, a poetic genre originating in tenth-century Muslim Iberia and adopted by poets writing in Hebrew as well as Arabic. The kharjas were lines of verse imported from other sources, including folk poetry, and some of them were written not in Arabic or Hebrew but in Ibero-Romance. Like the cantigas de amigo, the

Ibero-Romance kharjas are typically narrated by a girl in love. They are among the oldest examples of the ancient Romance language spoken on the peninsula.

Whether or not a remote connection exists between the kharja and the cantiga de amigo, it is inconceivable that the Galician-Portuguese troubadours invented this latter genre out of thin air—which is to say, solely on the basis of what they learned from Occitan troubadours, who knew no such genre. All the more curious, then, that the first generation or two of Galician-Portuguese poets wrote mostly cantigas de amor, some satiric poems, and only an occasional cantiga de amigo. This last type of love song grew popular only as time went on. Perhaps the Occitan canso—refashioned as the cantiga de amor—initially attracted most of the attention for being a novelty item, with local troubadours only later turning to and transforming their native lyric traditions. Those pre-troubadour traditions may also have included love poetry narrated by men—to judge by an early, not at all typical cantiga de amor, "You who from Montemaior have come" (no. 3), with incantatory, repeating lines and an exceptionally long refrain.

The Galician-Portuguese troubadours used native song traditions for their own purpose, which was to make imaginative, entertaining works for their aristocratic sponsors and for their own delight. While some of the earlier cantigas de amigo are naïve enough, there is nothing innocent about the girl in cantiga 96 who doesn't believe a word of the suitor who supposedly wants a private meeting "to simply talk." The speaker in cantiga 97, resembling not a simple girl in love but the haughty lady we find in cantigas de amor, declares that her lover's praise is only to be expected, because she's good-looking and deserves it. And the narrator of cantiga 25 also strikes us as an experienced woman, who warns others never to believe the suitor who claims to be dying of love, though she'd be glad to see one literally drop dead. On the other hand, the troubadours sometimes sing their own praises through the voice of the narrating girl, as in cantiga

45, where she brags about her boyfriend's skill as both a lyricist and a composer. These and many other cantigas de amigo owed as much to the troubadours' own ingenuity as to any indigenous lyric form.

The more than four hundred satirical songs known as *cantigas de escárnio e maldizer* lack the lyrical charm of the cantigas de amigo and the technical refinement achieved in the best cantigas de amor, but their thematic content and occasional outrageousness make them every bit as entertaining as the two genres of love songs. Love songs, appropriately enough, are one of the butts of their mockery. Pero Garcia Burgalês, for example, marvels at a fellow troubadour's ability to repeatedly die in his cantigas de amor and resurrect, just like Jesus, on the third day (no. 33). (Dying because of love, it must be said, was a stunt that commenced with the Occitan poets, though they did not abuse it so much.) And Joam Garcia de Guilhade, when hounded by a lady for a cantiga de amor, complied with a song (no. 28) that begins:

> Ugly lady, you've complained
> that I never sing your praise,
> so I've composed a new refrain
> to sing your praise in my own way,
> and this is what my song exclaims:
> you're a crazy, old, and ugly lady!

The aforementioned fragmentary treatise on the Galician-Portuguese troubadours' art describes two different kinds of satiric compositions: the openly slanderous cantiga de maldizer, which uses transparent language, referring directly to its target, and the veiled cantiga de escárnio, which relies on double entendres and insinuation to ridicule its victim. In practice it's not always easy to distinguish between the two types, and most scholars group all the satiric verse together, often under the general heading *cantigas de escárnio*. But the fact that these subdivisions existed, along with some other terminology for the satirical songs that I won't get into here, makes us wonder if this genre, like the cantigas de amigo, had an ancient history.

When directed at individuals, some of the Occitan sirventes could be scathing, but on the whole they can't compare with the cantigas de escárnio for sarcasm, vitriol, irreverence, and obscenity. Manuel Rodrigues Lapa (1897–1989), who produced the first complete edition of the cantigas de escárnio, called their ensemble a "moral sewer,"[5] suggesting a certain priggishness, but many a reader might blush at Afonso Anes do Cotom's wonderment that a woman named Marinha doesn't explode from the impact of his sexual parts so completely filling hers (no. 12; a Marinha also appears in cantiga 120), or at Pero Garcia Burgalês's account of Maria Negra, who goes broke from buying penises that rot as soon as she "sticks them" into "her smelly stable" (no. 36). The cantigas de escárnio also took aim at homosexuals, prostitutes, lascivious nuns and priests, and tedious or dull-witted individuals. But not all was sex and scurrility. There are songs that denounce the avarice and laziness of noblemen, as well as the corruption and hypocrisy of church officials.

Some cantigas are hybrids and resist classification. Cantiga 103, for instance, because of its brevity, its setting, and its use of the purest, most primitive form of parallelism, is in every respect a cantiga de amigo except for its male point of view, which makes it count as a cantiga de amor. Still other cantigas don't fit into any of the three main genres, not even as hybrids. A few troubadours wrote songs that, reflecting on the worsening state of the world, resemble the moral sirvente of Occitan poetry. Another poem type imported from France, the pastoral song, presents a shepherdess in dialogue with the troubadour, or she soliloquizes while he looks on in silence.

◆ ◆ ◆

[5] Lapa, *Lições de Literatura Portuguesa*, 161.

20

Although composed, in all likelihood, by a group of troubadours under the direction of Alfonso X, the *Cantigas de Santa Maria* don't really qualify as troubadour poetry, and not only because of their very different subject matter. Enormous stylistic differences also separate one kind of poetry from the other. Most of the Marian cantigas are narrative, make no use of parallelism, and have longish lines, often with fourteen or more syllables. Nearly all of them have refrains, as do a majority of the secular cantigas, but the predominant strophic form of the *Cantigas de Santa Maria* was inspired by the *zajal*, a type of Arabic Andalusian song in dialect that somewhat resembles the French virelay. The several hundred zajal-like cantigas in honor of Mary begin with a refrain, whose rhyme is echoed in the last line of each stanza, in a scheme such as *AAbbba* or *AAbba* (where *AA* is the refrain). Very few examples of this sort of stanzaic form can be found among the 1,680 secular cantigas. And the metrical structures typical of the cantigas de amigo or cantigas de amor are, in turn, equally rare in the Marian cantigas.

It's worth remembering that the Occitan troubadours (whose ranks included many clerics) also composed devotional songs. These were lyric expressions of their own particular sensibilities, however, rather than made-to-order contributions to someone else's project.

The pet literary project of Alfonso X's later life, the Marian songbook was successively enlarged, from one hundred to two hundred to four hundred cantigas, most of which were composed between 1265 and 1282. As the collection grew, the songs were reordered to accommodate various numerical schemes. At the first doubling, for example, numbers ending in 5 were assigned to the longer songs. In all three versions, the numbers ending in 0 correspond to hymns of praise and supplication, with a shorter line and generally fewer stanzas than the narrative songs recounting miracles. And in the final version, the songs whose numbers end in 00 feature the first-person voice of Alfonso X.

Collections of miracles attributed to Mary and recorded in Latin became somewhat of a fad in the eleventh century. With the emergence of the preaching orders—the Franciscans in 1209 and the Dominicans in 1216—religious writings began to appear in vernacular tongues, and major miracle collections were produced in French by Gautier de Coincy (1177–1236), in Castilian Spanish by Berceo (ca. 1198–ca. 1264), and in Galician-Portuguese by Alfonso X. This last was by far the largest vernacular collection, chronicling more than 350 miracles. The stories were drawn from miracle collections in Latin, from collections associated with shrines in France and Iberia, and from local oral traditions.

Besides presenting a colorful panorama of typical as well as eccentric individuals from various social strata and from various countries, the *Cantigas de Santa Maria* offer some surprising glimpses into medieval religiosity and moral attitudes. Telling examples are when the Virgin cures a sick monk by giving him milk from her breast, when she helps two robbers break jail because they promised to contribute nails to a shrine, and when she refills an empty wine vat for the benefit of drunk pilgrims who wanted to get drunker.[6]

Music for virtually all the Marian cantigas has thankfully been preserved in songbooks produced in Alfonso X's scriptorium. A miniature at the beginning of one of the more lavishly decorated songbooks depicts the king seated on his throne and flanked by two scribes, one of whom is writing while the other looks up from his parchment to listen. The monarch is glancing at an open book and appears to be dictating. To his far left there is a group of four clerics (singers?) examining a text, and to his far right a group of three musicians, probably jongleurs. Even if this isn't an accurate picture of how the songs were composed, it confirms that they were created through a team effort, with the king leading the team. There is pretty good evidence that Airas Nunes, a Galician cleric and masterful troubadour, was a

---

[6] Songs 54, 106, and 351, respectively, in Walter Mettmann's edition.

contributor to the *Cantigas de Santa Maria,* and we can take it for granted that he was assisted by other courtly troubadours, who were both fluent in Galician-Portuguese and proficient versifiers.

But Alfonso X did not merely coordinate the work of others. Close to forty of the Marian songs allude to his family, his court, and events in his own life, suggesting that he himself was their author. By weaving so many personal details into the project, the king configured his life—for posterity—as a fundamentally spiritual journey.

◆ ◆ ◆

Given the central place of the Virgin Mary in the medieval imagination, it would be logical to assume that the songs included in the *Cantigas de Santa Maria* were destined for the general public, but it seems they never spread far beyond Alfonso's court. Despite all the resources allocated to composing and preserving the Marian cantigas, little effort was made to disseminate them. The reasons for this may have been circumstantial. The last few years of the king's reign were a fraught period, in which his son Sancho, backed by large swaths of the nobility and part of the church hierarchy, rebelled against him, making it hard if not impossible for him to promote the use of his cantigas in public worship. It's not entirely clear, however, that he especially wanted to promote them among the masses of faithful Catholics. Given that the people in his kingdom, Castile, spoke a related but different language, they might not have been receptive to devotional songs written in Galician-Portuguese. Whether by design or by chance, the *Cantigas de Santa Maria* were a religious poetry for an elite, ironically relying on popular sources for their narrative content.

The secular poetry of the troubadours was even less likely to leave court. A few of the cantigas de escárnio may have circulated as propaganda on behalf of certain policy goals, such as the recruitment of soldiers for the Reconquista against the Moors, but what audience could courtly love poetry have found outside the immediate context that defined it? Troubadour poetry on the peninsula had a small audience, much smaller than in southern France, where there was a comparatively extensive network of noble courts, and this may be one of the reasons the Galician-Portuguese cantigas—subject to less critical review—were less impressive than the cansos and sirventes of Occitania.

I've been using the word *troubadour* broadly, to indicate any author of what we call troubadour poetry, or song, but some of the authors in fact had a lower social status, that of jongleur (*jograr* in Galician-Portuguese), a term that can conjure visions of accomplished musicians but also of jesters and jugglers. Confusion surrounding these terms existed already in the thirteenth century and prompted the troubadour Guiraut Riquier, who had lived for many years in Alfonso X's court, to address a poetic *suplicatio* to the king, begging him to clearly define the different roles played by the troubadour and the jongleur. Acceding to the request, the king issued a *declaratio* (written in Occitan by Riquier) in which he distinguished between various categories of composers and performers. Veritable troubadours, he stipulated, authored both the lyrics and the melodies of court poetry, and the best among them merited the title "doctor in the art of troubadour poetry." (Merited or not, no such title existed.) The court jongleur, on the other hand, was essentially a performer, singing what the troubadour composed, but he was not to be confused with the street jongleurs. Some of the street jongleurs were talented singers, admitted the king, but they lacked the necessary refinement to be accepted at court, so that it would be better to call them "buffoons," the name used in Lombardy for those who tamed monkeys, handled marionettes, imitated birds, and played the fool.

Some of the jongleurs were attached to a court, while others worked on a freelance basis, singing songs by sundry authors and receiving compensation from the nobles they entertained. And besides the male jongleurs, or *jograres*, there were female *jograresas*, more commonly called *solda-deiras*, since they were paid in *soldos* (a unit of currency) for their performances, which included singing, playing musical instruments, and dancing. They were also reputed to be available for sex. A number of cantigas de escárnio mock the concupiscent behavior of soldadeiras such as Marinha (no. 12) and, especially, the notorious Maria Perez Balteira (nos. 17 and 72). This scoffing, however misogynistic, probably reflects the professional reality of these women, expected to dispense sexual favors as part of their job. Then too, the sexual mores among these performance artists, whatever their gender, seem not to have been especially strict.

Occasionally a jongleur was in the employ of a single troubadour, performing his songs and in some cases helping to compose the words or music. Juião Bolseiro and other jongleurs who composed their own songs were effectively troubadours, but upstarts often endured abuse from their class-conscious colleagues. Lourenço, a jongleur in the service of Joam Garcia de Guilhade, had to repeatedly defend himself against insults heaped on him by his master and by other troubadours, who found fault with the cantigas he composed.

More than a dozen females—*trobairitz*—produced cansos and sirventes in Occitania, but while it's possible that a few Iberian soldadeiras composed their own songs, the cantigas that have come down to us were all written by men, a majority of them aristocrats, some clerics, and still others (jongleurs) commoners.

◆ ◆ ◆

The cantigas de amor, de amigo, and de escárnio circulated on loose sheets or scrolls for the benefit of the jongleurs who sang them and for the kings and nobles who were the troubadours' patrons. Individual songbooks were made for the cantigas of King Alfonso X, King Dinis, and possibly a few other troubadours. The songs from these various sources were subsequently compiled into anthological cancioneiros, two of which have survived, either in their original form or in copies.

The *Cancioneiro de Ajuda*, discovered around the year 1800 and at present kept in the library of the Ajuda Palace in Lisbon, seems to date from the very end of the thirteenth century. Although space for music was left below the first stanza of each cantiga, no musical notation was inscribed therein. The unfinished songbook includes 310 cantigas, virtually all of them cantigas de amor, with no indication of who composed them, but 246 of the songs can be found in one or both of the other cancioneiros, where the authors are duly identified.

Both the *Cancioneiro da Biblioteca Nacional* (housed in Portugal's National Library) and the *Cancioneiro da Vaticana* (in the Vatican Library) were copied in the early sixteenth century from an older, now lost cancioneiro at the behest of the Italian humanist Angelo Colocci, who made occasional notes in the margins. No space was left for the music. Discovered in 1840, the Vatican songbook contains around twelve hundred cantigas, while the songbook belonging to the National Library of Portugal, discovered in 1878, contains some 1,560 cantigas.

Of the several surviving folios and fragments with Galician-Portuguese cantigas, two are especially important. The Vindel Parchment, named after the Spanish bookseller who discovered it in 1913 or 1914 in the binding of a fourteenth-century codex, contains the seven cantigas de amigo composed by Martim Codax (nos. 60–66), with musical notation for all but the sixth. The manuscript dates from the thirteenth century and is now housed at the Pierpont Morgan Library of New York. No less significant for the history of music is the Sharrer Parchment, belonging to the Portuguese National Archives and discovered in 1990 by Harvey L. Sharrer, an American professor and researcher. It is a single folio containing fragmentary text and musical notation for seven cantigas de amor by King Dinis, and it once belonged to a volume of large dimensions, probably produced by scribes connected to Dinis's court.

The manuscript tradition of the *Cantigas de Santa Maria* is far more straightforward. Four surviving song collections—three of them with musical notation—were produced under Alfonso X's supervision. One of the collections is in Florence; the other three are in Spanish libraries. A curiosity: among the first 149 folios of the second collection of Marian cantigas (housed in the library of El Escorial), the only one missing is the fortieth, which contained a song of praise to the Virgin Mary that appears, anomalously, amid the secular cantigas of Alfonso included in the *Cancioneiro da Biblioteca Nacional.* We can imagine a filing error in the king's busy scriptorium, with the folio having been inadvertently inserted into a collection of his nonreligious cantigas and later copied into the larger, anthological songbooks.

◆ ◆ ◆

Although words were central to the troubadours' art, music was an essential vehicle for conveying the words to the listener and enhancing their effect. Some of the cantigas—which were sung by solo voices, with or without musical accompaniment—must have been appreciated more for their melodies than for their words, so more's the pity that hardly any music for secular Galician-Portuguese troubadour poetry has survived. But the thirteen musically notated cantigas discovered in the twentieth century, despite providing models for just a handful of verse schemes, have allowed musicologists to make a few general observations. The Martim Codax cantigas de amigo appearing in the Vindel Parchment have simple strophic schemes, and their likewise short-range, rhapsodic melodies seem to confirm a preexisting tradition of popular song that was co-opted by jongleurs and eventually the troubadours. The Sharrer Manuscript, on the other hand, presents comparatively sophisticated melodic lines for its seven cantigas de amor by King

Dinis, with larger intervals and with more notes per syllable than in the Codax cantigas. The music for the Dinis songs is more elevated and less emotional, denoting influences from France but with its own musical originality. That said, King Dinis and his Galician-Portuguese peers produced more than a few *contrafacta*—cantigas de amor as well as cantigas de escárnio that were set to the music of Occitan or French troubadour songs. They were following a practice that was common among troubadours all over Europe.

With over four hundred melodies taking many different forms—zajal, rondeau, rondel, ballad—the *Cantigas de Santa Maria* are an unusually rich compendium and have become popular among performers of ancient music, compensating for the centuries-long neglect they fell into immediately after being composed. Musically speaking, these cantigas have a few points in common with their secular counterpart, evincing some influence from France, but they were more decisively influenced by Arabic Andalusian models.

I don't dare venture into the technical aspects of cantiga music, but I urge readers to listen to performance recordings of the cantigas by Martim Codax and King Dinis (available through the site *Cantigas medievais galego-portuguesas*) and of the *Cantigas de Santa Maria* (available through numerous internet sites).

The secular cantigas, quite apart from their musical significance, are the founding texts of two national literatures. Galician literature would soon languish in the so-called *séculos escuros*, the dark centuries, before reemerging in the 1800s, with the cantigas serving as crucial evidence of its ancient pedigree and poetic richness. The literature of Portugal, although it went through some dull periods, has generated a steady stream of poetry, drama, and prose, and a few of its writers, such as Luís Vaz de Camões, rank among Europe's finest. In the cantigas we can note certain qualities that would become hallmarks of Portuguese literature. I'm thinking in particular of King Dinis's observation that the Occitan poets were better crafters of verse but that he and other writers of cantigas felt love more truly and sincerely. Already back then, a myth about the intensity and authenticity of Portuguese feeling was taking shape, and its consequences for the future of Portuguese literature were not always felicitous, since overt and unmediated sincerity quickly turns maudlin. It seems absurd to suppose that Portuguese people might feel more, or more ardently, than other people, but because that myth has been ingrained into the national psyche, it may be responsible for having made some writers more acutely *aware* of what they immediately feel. Whatever its exact origin, that awareness has certainly contributed to the greatness of poets such as Camões and Pessoa.

A companion myth to the Portuguese capacity-for-feeling myth is *saudade*, a reputedly untranslatable word that denotes melancholic longing, yearning, or nostalgia. The word, which also exists in modern Galician but not in Spanish, occurs for the first time in the cantigas, where it is spelled *soidade*. Longing and nostalgia are of course universal sentiments, but the Portuguese, who still today wax nostalgic for the age when their navigators ruled the seas, have turned saudade into a national leitmotif and philosophy of life. Perhaps it could not have been otherwise. Perhaps saudade is in fact a remote inheritance from illiterate young women in western Iberia who dreamed of a better life and an enchanting love while washing clothes at the stream and singing, in a wistful voice, cantigas de amigo.[7]

---

[7] For my discussion of the origins of the cantigas, I'm indebted to António Resende de Oliveira and José António Souto Cabo. Resende de Oliveira has amassed evidence to support the idea that the cantigas de amor partly reflected a real frustration of aristocratic troubadours practically obliged to remain celibate. Giuseppe Tavani first stressed how the cantigas de amigo are, in certain respects, the converse of the cantigas de amor. I owe my summary observations on the music of the cantigas to Manuel Pedro Ferreira.

Notes on the Text and Translation

The spelling of Galician-Portuguese was inconsistent, to put it mildly, and the copyists of the cancioneiros—working under pressure—occasionally garbled a phrase, or they abbreviated words and repeated lines in such a way as to obscure the author's intentions. Scholars have arrived at a consensus about what the individual lines for most of the cantigas say, but their methods for transcribing them and standardizing the spelling vary widely. This book presents the cantigas as they appear on the online database *Cantigas medievais galego-portuguesas*, where modern Portuguese spelling conventions have been used to represent the sounds of Galician-Portuguese. This means that most double consonants and some double vowels have been eliminated; the letters *y* and *j*, when used as vowels with the sound of *i*, have been replaced by *i*; the silent *h* has been dropped from some words but added to others; and nasalized vowels, usually denoted in the cancioneiros by a tilde or by an unpronounced *n* following the vowel (for instance, *bẽ* or *ben*) have usually been transcribed with an unpronounced *m* following the vowel (*bem*), as in modern Portuguese. In addition to these and other changes in spelling, the editors of the database have spelled out the copyists' frequent abbreviations. The resulting transcriptions have the great advantage of allowing readers with some knowledge of Portuguese to better grasp the meaning and pronunciation of the ancient language. For a more conservative approach to transcription, readers can consult the Galician online database *Universo cantigas*, where the work of editing the cantigas is still in progress. Both databases provide glossaries and prose summaries (in Portuguese and Galician) for many of the cantigas, as well as information on their original sources. The Portuguese database includes facsimile images of those sources.

Punctuation, practically nonexistent in the cancioneiros, is added by modern editors in accord with their interpretations and personal taste. I have taken the liberty of slightly altering the punctuation proposed by the editors at *Cantigas medievais galego-portuguesas*, and in a few cantigas I have preferred a slightly different reading of the original manuscripts. Scholars typically use brackets to indicate editorial additions—including words to fill in the presumed lapses of copyists—but I have opted for a cleaner presentation of the original texts. Mettmann's edition is my source for three songs from the *Cantigas de Santa Maria*. The genre given for each cantiga (de amor, de amigo, de escárnio) is deduced from its style and thematic content. For songs that reflect on the world at large in a moral tone I have used the term *cantiga moral*.

My ordering of the cantigas is vaguely chronological. The four authors of cantigas 1–7 were definitely among the earliest troubadours, and those whose cantigas appear after King Dinis's were among the last. For most of the troubadours in between, it is often difficult to ascertain the exact period when they were poetically active, and in a few cases nothing at all is known about them for sure. The biographical information at the back of this volume has been drawn from the far more detailed sketches found at *Cantigas medievais galego-portuguesas*, whose editors are constantly updating their database thanks to the research of numerous scholars in the field.

The notes to the poems indicate where my translations have strayed from the literal sense of the original. The titles are my own invention (none of the cantigas had titles), and the protesting reader is invited to rub them out.

Acknowledgments

Elsa Gonçalves was my trusty guide when I first entered the world of the cantigas, more than thirty years ago. João Dionísio and Ângela Correia also advised me and answered questions as I found my way. The John Simon Guggenheim Memorial Foundation supported my translations with a fellowship.

For this new edition, Graça Videira Lopes and Manuel Pedro Ferreira have graciously allowed me to reproduce the cantiga transcriptions found at the database *Cantigas medievais galego-portuguesas*. They also offered valuable suggestions for my introduction. Martin Earl thoroughly read the initial draft of the introduction and made, as usual, no small number of incisive observations. I'm grateful to Peter Cole, Martin Earl, Richard Sieburth, and Rosanna Warren for their generous, comprehensive review of the manuscript

The Cantigas

1.

OSOIRO ANES

cantiga de amor

Cuidei eu de meu coraçom
que me nom podesse forçar,
pois me sacara de prisom,
e d'ir comego i tornar.
E forçou-m'ora nov'amor,
e forçou-me nova senhor;
e cuido ca me quer matar.

E pois me assi desemparar
ũa senhor foi, des entom
eu cuidei bem per rem que nom
podesse mais outra cobrar.
Mais forçarom-mi os olhos meus
e o bom parecer dos seus
e o seu preç'e um cantar

que lh'oí, u a vi estar
em cabelos, dizend'um som.
Mal dia nom morri entom,
ante que tal coita levar
qual levo, que nom vi maior
nunca, ond'estou a pavor
de morte, ou de lho mostrar!

34

1.

OSOIRO ANES

Song of a Man Gone Back to Prison

I never thought my heart
could ever force me back
into the prison of passion
I'd only lately departed.
It forced on me a new love
and forced on me a new lady
to make me, I fear, love's martyr.

Having once suffered great pain
because of a lady I loved,
I thought I could never be moved
to fall in love again.
But I've been forced by my eyes
and the beauty in hers that shine,
by her virtue and a refrain

I heard her sing when her hair
was uncovered. Unlucky day!
I wish I'd been given death
instead of having to bear
this heartache, so severe
that I sincerely fear
I must die or my love declare.

2.

cantiga de amor

Mim prês forçadament'Amor,
e fez-mi amar quem nunc'amou;
e fez-mi tort'e desamor
que mi atal senhor tornou.
E vejo que mal baratei
que mi a tal senhor tornei,
que nom sabe que é amar,
e sab'a homem penas dar.

Que forçad'hoj'e sem sabor
eno mundo vivendo vou,
ca nunca púdi haver sabor
de mim nem d'al, des que foi sou,
senom dela. E que farei?
Por que pregunto? Ca eu sei:
viver hei, se de mim pensar,
ou morrer, se mim nom amar!

Quem quer x'esto pode veer
(e mais quem mego vid'houer):
que nom hei já sem, nem poder
de m'emparar d'ũa molher,
a mais mansa que nunca vi,
nem mais sem sanha, pois naci.
Veed'ora se estou mal,
que m'emparar nom sei de tal.

. . .

36

2.

OSOIRO ANES

Song about Love's Injustice

Love brutally took hold of me,
bestowing, instead of love, injustice
by making me love a certain lady
who in all her life has never loved.
I see that I've only won disgrace
by loving a lady such as this:
a lady to whom love makes no sense,
who can break a heart with indifference.

In this world, without enjoyment,
I have no choice but to endure,
as it's not in my power to enjoy
myself or anything else but her,
my lady and lord. So what now?
Why do I ask? I already know:
I'll live, if she cares a little for me,
or die, if she doesn't love me!

As anyone can easily see
(more so if they spend time with me)
I've lost my reason and the means
to defend myself against a woman
who of all the women I've seen
is the meekest and most serene.
Look at me tremble before such as she
and judge for yourself if I can be happy.

. . .

Ca sõo tam em seu poder
que, se end'al fazer quiser,
non'o poderei eu fazer,
se m'ende Deus poder nom der
contra ela, que eu servi,
qual dou a ela sobre mi.
Que nunca eu soub'amar al,
ergo ela que mi faz mal.

By this woman I'm so enchanted
that I can't even try
to react, unless God grants me
the power to resist her, since I,
a smitten servant, have granted her
the power to rule me: I'm at her mercy.
I've never been able to love another
woman but her, who makes me suffer.

3.

GIL SANCHES

cantiga de amor

Tu, que ora vens de Montemaior,
tu, que ora vens de Montemaior,
digas-me mandado de mia senhor,
digas-me mandado de mia senhor;
    ca se eu seu mandado
    nom vir, trist'e coitado
    serei; e gram pecado
    fará, se me nom val;
    ca em tal hora nado
    foi que, mao-pecado!
    amo-a endoado,
    e nunca end'houvi al.

Tu, que ora viste os olhos seus,
tu, que ora viste os olhos seus,
digas-me mandado dela, por Deus,
digas-me mandado dela, por Deus;
    ca se eu seu mandado
    nom vir, trist'e coitado
    serei; e gram pecado
    fará, se me nom val;
    ca em tal hora nado
    foi que, mao-pecado!
    amo-a endoado,
    e nunca end'houvi al.

3.

GIL SANCHES

Song for a Word from Montemaior

You who from Montemaior have come,
you who from Montemaior have come,
give me a word from the lady I love,
give me a word from the lady I love,
    since if she hasn't sent
    any word, I'll be upset
    and sadly regret
    how I've been slighted,
    born on a day
    that doomed me to the pain
    of loving her in vain,
    my passion unrequited.

You who've just now seen her eyes,
you who've just now seen her eyes,
give me a word, by God on high,
give me a word, by God on high,
    since if she hasn't sent
    any word, I'll be upset
    and sadly regret
    how I've been slighted,
    born on a day
    that doomed me to the pain
    of loving her in vain,
    my passion unrequited.

4.

FERNÃO RODRIGUES DE CALHEIROS

cantiga de amigo

Madre, passou per aqui um cavaleiro
e leixou-me namorad'e com marteiro.
   Ai madre, os seus amores hei!
     Se me los hei,
     ca mi os busquei,
     outros me lhe dei.
   Ai madre, os seus amores hei!

Madre, passou per aqui um filho d'algo
e leixou-m'assi penada com'eu ando,
   Ai madre, os seus amores hei!
     Se me los hei,
     ca mi os busquei,
     outros me lhe dei.
   Ai madre, os seus amores hei!

Madre, passou per aqui quem nom passasse,
e leixou-m'assi penada, mais leixasse;
   Ai madre, os seus amores hei!
     Se me los hei,
     ca mi os busquei,
     outros me lhe dei.
   Ai madre, os seus amores hei!

4.

FERNÃO RODRIGUES DE CALHEIROS

Song of a Girl Who Sought Love

Mother, it was here I chanced to meet a lord,
who left me in love and yearning with sorrow.
   Oh, Mother, how I'm in love!
     If I'm in love,
      it's because I sought it,
      but he also caught it.
   Oh, Mother, how I'm in love!

Mother, it was here I met a nobleman
who left me in this troubled mood.
   Oh, Mother, how I'm in love!
     If I'm in love,
      it's because I sought it,
      but he also caught it.
   Oh, Mother, how I'm in love!

Mother, it was here—had it only not been!—
that he left me with this painful longing.
   Oh, Mother, how I'm in love!
     If I'm in love,
      it's because I sought it,
      but he also caught it.
   Oh, Mother, how I'm in love!

5.

FERNÃO RODRIGUES DE CALHEIROS

cantiga de amigo

Que farei agor', amigo,
pois que nom queredes migo
    viver?
    Ca nom poss'eu al bem querer.

Em gram coita me leixades,
se vós alhur ir cuidades
    viver,
    ca nom poss'eu al bem querer.

Se aquesta ida vossa
for, nom sei eu como possa
    viver,
    ca nom poss'eu al bem querer.

Matar-mi-ei, se mi o dizedes
que vós rem sem mi podedes
    viver,
    ca nom poss'eu al bem querer.

5.

FERNÃO RODRIGUES DE CALHEIROS

Song for a Friend Who's Going Away

What will I do, my friend,
if with me you don't intend
    to live?
        I want nothing else in life.

You'll cause me great distress
if you go anywhere else
    to live,
        as I want nothing else in life.

If indeed you're leaving,
I don't know how I'll keep on
    living,
        as I want nothing else in life.

Kill myself is what I'll do
if without me you
    can live,
        as I want nothing else in life.

6.

PAIO SOARES DE TAVEIRÓS

cantiga de amor

Como morreu quem nunca bem
houve da rem que mais amou,
e quem viu quanto receou
dela, e foi morto por en:
    ai, mia senhor, assi moir'eu!

Como morreu quem foi amar
quem lhe nunca quis bem fazer,
e de que lhe fez Deus veer
de que foi morto com pesar:
    ai, mia senhor, assi moir'eu!

Com'home que ensandeceu,
senhor, com gram pesar que viu
e nom foi ledo nem dormiu
depois, mia senhor, e morreu:
    ai, mia senhor, assi moir'eu!

Como morreu quem amou tal
dona que lhe nunca fez bem,
e quen'a viu levar a quem
a nom valia, nen'a val:
    ai, mia senhor, assi moir'eu!

6.

PAIO SOARES DE TAVEIRÓS

Song of How I Die

Like one who died because he never
won the woman he most loved
but saw her do what he most dreaded
and so no longer wished to live,
   that, dear lady, is how I die!

Like one who died for having adored
a woman who never showed him favor
but did, by God, what he most abhorred,
making his life lose all its flavor,
   that, dear lady, is how I die!

Like one, dear lady, who lost his mind
because of the dreadful thing he saw,
and then, unable to sleep or find
any joy in life, could not go on,
   that, dear lady, is how I die!

Like one who died for loving a woman
without ever seeing his love returned
and saw her, instead, take up with a man
who didn't and doesn't deserve her,
   that, dear lady, is how I die!

7.

PAIO SOARES DE TAVEIRÓS

cantiga de amor

No mundo nom me sei parelh'
mentre me for como me vai,
ca já moiro por vós e ai,
mia senhor branc'e vermelha,
queredes que vos retraia
quando vos eu vi em saia?
Mao dia me levantei
que vos entom nom vi fea!

E ai!, mia senhor, des aquelh'
dia, me foi a mi mui lai.
E vós, filha de dom Paai
Moniz, e bem vos semelha
d'haver eu por vós garvaia?
Pois eu, mia senhor, d'alfaia
nunca de vós houve nem hei
valia d'ũa correa.

7.

PAIO SOARES DE TAVEIRÓS

Song to a Lady in Simple Clothes

I don't know a soul whose plight
compares with my unhappy affair:
I'm dying for your love, I swear,
and you, whose cheeks are rosy white,
want me to paint you well composed,
when I saw you in simple clothes.
I wish I'd stayed in bed that day
or found you less attractive!

Yes, dear lady, from that day since,
I've known only unhappiness.
And you, daughter of Paio Moniz,
act as if you were convinced
that you bestowed on me a robe
when from you I've had no clothes
and never had, beloved lady,
so much as a flimsy strap.

8.

LOPO

cantiga de amigo

—Filha, se gradoedes,
dizede que havedes.
  —Nom mi dam amores vagar.

—Filha, se bem hajades,
dized'e nom mençades.
  —Nom mi dam amores vagar.

—Dizede, pois vos mando,
por que ides chorando.
  —Nom mi dam amores vagar.

Par Sam Leuter vos digo:
cuidand'em meu amigo,
  nom mi dam amores vagar.

8.

LOPO

Song of a Restless Heart

Daughter, if I may ask,
tell me what's the matter.
My heart is all unrest.

Daughter, if you please,
tell me what this means.
My heart is all unrest.

Give a straight reply!
Why is it you're crying?
My heart is all unrest.

I swear by St. Eleutherius:
thinking about my lover,
my heart is all unrest.

9.

MARTIM SOARES

cantiga de escárnio

Foi um dia Lopo jograr
a cas d'um infançom cantar;
e mandou-lh'ele por dom dar
três couces na garganta;
e fui-lh'escass', a meu cuidar,
segundo com'el canta.

Escasso foi o infançom
em seus couces partir em dom,
ca nom deu a Lopo, entom,
mais de três na garganta;
e mais merece o jograrom,
segundo com'el canta.

9.

MARTIM SOARES

Song about Lopo the Jongleur

Lopo the jongleur one day went
to sing at the house of a nobleman,
who ordered that he get as payment
three swift kicks below his chin,
which was stingy in my opinion,
    considering how he sings.

The nobleman was much too stingy
in the number of kicks he ordered,
with Lopo only being given
three of them below his chin;
that joke of a jongleur deserved more,
    considering how he sings.

10.

MARTIM SOARES

cantiga de amor

Senhor fremosa, pois me nom queredes
creer a coita 'm que me tem Amor,
por meu mal é que tam bem parecedes
e por meu mal vos filhei por senhor
e por meu mal tam muito bem oí
dizer de vós e por meu mal vos vi:
pois meu mal é quanto bem vós havedes.

E pois vos vós da coita nom nembrades,
nem do afã que mi o Amor faz sofrer,
por meu mal vivo mais ca vós cuidades
e por meu mal me fezo Deus nacer
e por meu mal nom morri u cuidei
como vos viss'e por meu mal fiquei
vivo, pois vós por meu mal rem nom dades.

E desta coita 'm que me vós tẽedes,
em que hoj'eu vivo tam sem sabor,
que farei eu, pois mi a vós nom creedes?
Que farei eu, cativo, pecador?
Que farei eu, vivendo sempre assi?
Que farei eu, que mal dia naci?
Que farei eu, pois me vós nom valedes?

. . .

10.

MARTIM SOARES

Song to an Unbelieving Lady

Dear lady, since you don't believe
that Love is making me ache for you,
for me it's a curse that you're so beautiful,
and it's my curse to be serving you,
and it's my curse that I heard of your fame,
and it's my curse that I saw your face:
my curse is in your every grace.

Since you ignore how much I ache
because of Love's unending torment,
my curse is even worse than you think,
and it's my curse to have been born,
and it's my curse that I didn't die
the day I saw you and a curse that I
still live, since to my curse you're blind.

This affliction in which I live
without any joy is thanks to you.
What will I do, since you don't believe me?
What will I do, such a hapless fool?
What will I do, living life this way?
What will I do, regretting each birthday?
What will I do against your disdain?

. . .

E pois que Deus nom quer que me valhades,
nem me queirades mia coita creer,
que farei eu? Por Deus, que mi o digades!
Que farei eu, se logo nom morrer?
Que farei eu, se mais a viver hei?
Que farei eu, que conselh'i nom sei?
Que farei eu, que vós desemparades?

Since God Himself makes you disdain me,
and you won't believe my heart is aching,
what will I do? For God's sake, explain!
What will I do if I keep on living?
What will I do if I don't die soon?
What will I do? There's no solution!
What will I do, denied by you?

11.

AFONSO ANES DO COTOM

cantiga de escárnio

Abadessa, oí dizer
que érades mui sabedor
de tod'o bem; e, por amor
de Deus, querede-vos doer
de mim, que ogano casei,
que bem vos juro que nom sei
mais que um asno de foder.

Ca me fazem en sabedor
de vós que havedes bom sem
de foder e de tod'o bem,
ensinade-me mais, senhor,
como foda, ca o nom sei,
nem padre nem madre nom hei
que m'ensin'e fic'i pastor.

E se eu ensinado vou
de vós, senhor, deste mester
de foder e foder souber
per vós, que me Deus aparou,
cada que per foder direi
Pater Noster e enmentarei
a alma de quem m'ensinou.

...

11.

AFONSO ANES DO COTOM

Song to a Learned Abbess

According to what I've heard,
abbess, you're very learned
about all good things. For love
of God, please have mercy
on me, as I know nothing
more than an ass about fucking
and just this year got married.

I've heard that when it comes
to fucking and other good fun
you're a most learned nun,
so teach me how to fuck,
madam, as I'm untrained.
Having no parents to explain
these things, I'm a simpleton.

Now if by you I'm told
about the art of screwing,
and if I learn to do it
from you in your godly role
as abbess, each time I fuck
I'll say a solemn Our Father,
and I'll say it for your soul.

. . .

E per i podedes gaar,
mia senhor, o reino de Deus,
per ensinar os pobres seus
mais ca por outro jajũar,
e per ensinar a molher
coitada, que a vós veer,
senhor, que nom souber ambrar.

I'm certain, madam, that you
can thus attain God's kingdom:
by teaching all poor sinners
more than abstaining from food,
and by teaching all the women
who come to seek your wisdom
about how they should screw.

12.

AFONSO ANES DO COTOM

cantiga de escárnio

Marinha, ende folegares
tenh'eu por desaguisado,
e som mui maravilhado
de ti, por nom rebentares:
ca che tapo eu daquesta minha
boca a ta boca, Marinha;
e destes narizes meus
tapo eu, Marinha, os teus;
e das mias mãos as orelhas,
os olhos, das sobrencelhas;
tapo-t'ao primeiro sono
da mia pissa o teu cono,
e mi o nom veja nengum,
e dos colhões esse cũ.
Como nom rebentas, Marinha?

12.

AFONSO ANES DO COTOM

Song to a Woman Who Doesn't Burst

Marinha, it confounds me
how you're still able to breathe,
nor does your body burst,
which equally astounds me,
since with my mouth I cover
your mouth until you smother,
and with my nose I close
the nostrils of your nose,
and my hands cover your ears,
my eyebrows hide your eyes,
and when the first sleep comes
my cock fills your cunt,
and my balls your rear,
till in you I disappear.
Why don't you burst, Marinha?

13.

NUNO FERNANDES TORNEOL

cantiga de amigo

Levad', amigo, que dormides as manhanas frias.
Tôdalas aves do mundo d'amor diziam.
Leda m'and'eu.

Levad', amigo que dormide'las frias manhanas.
Tôdalas aves do mundo d'amor cantavam.
Leda m'and'eu.

Tôdalas aves do mundo d'amor diziam;
do meu amor e do vosso em ment'haviam.
Leda m'and'eu.

Tôdalas aves do mundo d'amor cantavam;
do meu amor e do vosso i enmentavam.
Leda m'and'eu.

Do meu amor e do vosso em ment'haviam;
vós lhi tolhestes os ramos em que siíam.
Leda m'and'eu.

Do meu amor e do vosso i enmentavam;
vós lhi tolhestes os ramos em que pousavam.
Leda m'and'eu.

Vós lhi tolhestes os ramos em que siíam
e lhis secastes as fontes em que beviam.
Leda m'and'eu.

. . .

13.

Song for a Sleeping Lover

Rise up, beloved, who on cold mornings sleeps.
Birds the world over were singing of love.
    I'm a happy soul.

Rise up, beloved, who sleeps on cold mornings.
Love is what the world's birds were singing.
    I'm a happy soul.

Birds the world over were singing of love;
they had my love and yours in mind.
    I'm a happy soul.

Love is what the world's birds were singing;
their songs proclaimed my love and yours.
    I'm a happy soul.

They had my love and yours in mind;
you cut down the branches where they sat.
    I'm a happy soul.

Their songs proclaimed my love and yours;
you cut down the branches where they perched.
    I'm a happy soul.

You cut down the branches where they sat
and dried up the fountains where they drank.
    I'm a happy soul.

. . .

65

Vós lhi tolhestes os ramos em que pousavam
e lhis secastes as fontes u se banhavam.
Leda m'and'eu.

You cut down the branches where they perched
and dried up the fountains where they splashed.
    I'm a happy soul.

14.

NUNO FERNANDES TORNEOL

cantiga de amigo

Vi eu, mia madr', andar
as barcas eno mar,
   e moiro-me d'amor.

Foi eu, madre, veer
as barcas eno lez,
   e moiro-me d'amor.

As barcas eno mar
e foi-las aguardar,
   e moiro-me d'amor.

As barcas eno lez
e foi-las atender,
   e moiro-me d'amor.

E foi-las aguardar
e non'o pud'achar,
   e moiro-me d'amor.

E foi-las atender
e non'o pud'i veer,
   e moiro-me d'amor.

E non'o achei i,
o que por meu mal vi,
   e moiro-me d'amor.

14.

NUNO FERNANDES TORNEOL

Song about an Unarriving Lover

Mother, I have seen
the ships in from sea,
    and I'm dying of love.

Mother, I watched
the ships sail in,
    and I'm dying of love.

The ships in from sea,
I went to meet them,
    and I'm dying of love.

The ships sailed in,
I went and I waited,
    and I'm dying of love.

I went to meet them,
but nowhere could I see him,
    and I'm dying of love.

I went and I waited,
but I saw him nowhere,
    and I'm dying of love.

Nowhere could I see him
who causes my suffering,
    and I'm dying of love.

15.

cantiga de amor

Senhor do corpo delgado,
    em forte pont'eu fui nado,
que nunca perdi coidado
nem afã des que vos vi:
    em forte pont'eu fui nado,
    senhor, por vós e por mi!

Com est'afã tam longado,
    em forte pont'eu fui nado,
que vos amo sem meu grado
e faç'a vós pesar i:
    em forte pont'eu fui nado,
    senhor, por vós e por mi!

Ai eu, cativ'e coitado,
    em forte pont'eu fui nado,
que servi sempr'endõado
ond'um bem nunca prendi:
    em forte pont'eu fui nado,
    senhor, por vós e por mi!

15.

PERO DA PONTE

Song about a Bad Day

Oh lovely, graceful lady,
    I was born on a bad day.
Ever since you crossed my gaze
I'm restless, tense, and worried.
    I was born on a bad day,
    lady, for you and for me!

This worry never ends
    (I was born on a bad day),
since to love you I'm condemned
and you find my love annoying.
    I was born on a bad day,
    lady, for you and for me!

With a heart that won't quit aching,
    I was born on a bad day,
destined to serve in vain a lady
who never gave me anything.
    I was born on a bad day,
    lady, for you and for me!

16.

PERO DA PONTE

cantiga de amor

Se eu podesse desamar
a quem me sempre desamou
e podess'algum mal buscar
a quem me sempre mal buscou!
Assi me vingaria eu,
    se eu pudesse coita dar
    a quem me sempre coita deu.

Mais sol nom poss'eu enganar
meu coraçom que m'enganou,
per quanto mi fez desejar
a quem me nunca desejou.
E por esto nom dórmio eu,
    porque nom poss'eu coita dar
    a quem me sempre coita deu.

Mais rog'a Deus que desampar
a quem m'assi desamparou,
ou que podess'eu destorvar
a quem me sempre destorvou.
E logo dormiria eu,
    se eu podesse coita dar
    a quem me sempre coita deu.

. . .

16.

PERO DA PONTE

Song of a Lover Who Would Hate

If I could only learn to hate
the one who's always hated me!
If I could only make her hurt
for all the ways that she's hurt me!
I would have revenge at least
    if I could repay some of the grief
    to the woman who so grieved me.

But I can't even learn to fool
my very own heart. It fooled me
by making me completely fall
for one who'd never fall for me.
And this is why I never sleep:
    because I can't repay the grief
    to the woman who so grieved me.

I pray that God will yet reject
the one who always rejected me,
or that I'll make her feel upset
for all the times she upset me.
Then I'd finally sleep in peace
    if I could repay some of the grief
    to the woman who so grieved me.

. . .

Vel que ousass'en preguntar
a quem me nunca preguntou,
por que me fez em si cuidar,
pois ela nunca em mi cuidou.
E por esto lazeiro eu:
    porque nom posso coita dar
    a quem me sempre coita deu.

Or that I'll bring myself to ask
the one who never once asked me
why I've always thought of her,
though she's never thought of me!
And this is why I'm suffering:
    because I can't repay the grief
    to the woman who so grieved me.

17.

PERO DA PONTE

cantiga de escárnio

Maria Pérez, a nossa cruzada,
quando veo da terra d'Ultramar,
assi veo de perdom carregada
que se nom podia com el merger;
mais furtam-lho, cada u vai maer,
e do perdom já nom lhi ficou nada.

E o perdom é cousa mui preçada
e que se devia muit'a guardar;
mais ela nom há maeta ferrada
em que o guarde, nen'a pod'haver,
ca, pois o cadead'en foi perder,
sempr'a maeta andou descadeada.

Tal maeta como será guardada,
pois rapazes albergam no logar,
que nom haj'a seer mui trastornada?
Ca, o logar u eles ham poder,
nom há perdom que s'i possa asconder,
assi sabem trastornar a pousada.

E outra cousa vos quero dizer:
tal perdom bem se devera perder,
ca muito foi cousa mal gaada.

17.

PERO DA PONTE

Song about a Lost Crusade

On her return from the Holy Land
Maria Perez, our crusaderess,
carried so many indulgences
that she couldn't possibly sink,
but they were filched along the way
until not a single one remained.

Indulgences are a precious thing,
to be kept under lock and key,
but she didn't have a decent box
with a lock in which to keep them,
for ever since the lock was broken
her box has been left open.

How can a box like that be safe
in lodgings full of lusty fellows
who are sure to rifle through it?
In every place where they abound
there's no indulgence that won't be found:
they'll turn the hospice upside down!

There's one more thing I have to say:
those indulgences, obtained by fraud,
deserved to be taken away.

18.

cantiga de escárnio

Garcia López d'Elfaro,
direi-vos que m'agravece:
que vosso dom é mui caro
e vosso dom é rafece.
   O vosso dom é mui caro pera quen'o há d'haver,
   o vosso dom é rafece a quen'o há de vender.

Por caros teemos panos
que home pedir nom ousa,
e, poilos tragem dous anos
rafeces som, por tal cousa.
   O vosso dom é mui caro pera quen'o há d'haver,
   o vosso dom é rafece a quen'o há de vender.

Esto nunca eu cuidara:
que ũa cousa senlheira
podesse seer tam cara
e rafec'em tal maneira.
   O vosso dom é mui caro pera quen'o há d'haver,
   o vosso dom é rafece a quen'o há de vender.

18.

PERO DA PONTE

Song about Costly Cheap Goods

Garcia López de Alfaro
I'll tell you why I'm peeved:
the things you give are costly
but turn out to be cheap.
    Your gifts are costly for us to acquire,
    but cheap when sold, if we find a buyer.

Only through diligent service
can we earn your gift of cloths,
but since they're two years old,
they're cheap: they're full of moths.
    Your gifts are costly for us to acquire,
    but cheap when sold, if we find a buyer.

I never thought it possible
that one and the same thing
could be so very costly
and so extremely cheap.
    Your gifts are costly for us to acquire,
    but cheap when sold, if we find a buyer.

19.

PERO DA PONTE

cantiga de escárnio

Em almoeda vi estar
hoj'um ric'hom'e diss'assi:
—Quem quer um ric'home comprar?
E nunca i comprador vi
que o quisesse nem em dom,
ca diziam todos que nom
dariam um soldo por si.

E deste ric'home quem quer
vos pod'a verdade dizer:
pois nom há prês nẽum mester,
quem querrá i o seu perder?
Ca el nom faz nẽum lavor
de que nulh'hom'haja sabor,
nem sab'adubar de comer.

E u forom polo vender,
preguntarom-no em gram sem:
—Ric'hom', que sabedes fazer?
E o ric'home disse: —Rem.
Nom amo custa nem missom,
mais compro mui de coraçom
herdade, se mi a vend'alguém.

E pois el diss'esta razom,
nom houv'i molher nem barom
que por el dar quisesse rem.

19.

PERO DA PONTE

Song about a Nobleman Up for Auction

I saw a nobleman being auctioned
by a dealer who called out loud,
"What do I hear for a nobleman?"
but not a buyer could be found
who wanted him at any price.
"For that man there," they all cried,
"we wouldn't put a penny down."

Anyone there could tell you why
the auctioneer's task was futile:
the nobleman never learned a trade,
and who would pay for a useless fool?
He doesn't do any kind of labor
that might be a point in his favor,
nor can he fix the simplest food.

When they put him up for sale,
they wisely asked the man himself,
"Nobleman, what can you do?"
"Nothing," the nobleman said:
"I hate to work and hate to spend,
although I do like buying land,
if you have any you'd like to sell."

After they had heard all this,
not one man or woman present
offered the slightest pittance.

20.

PERO DA PONTE

cantiga de escárnio

Esta cantiga fez Pero da Ponte ao infante Dom Manuel, que se começa "E mort'é Martim Marcos", e na cobra segunda o podem entender.

Mort'é Dom Martim Marcos, ai Deus! Se é verdade
sei ca, se el é morto, morta é torpidade,
morta é bavequia e morta neiciidade,
morta é covardia e morta é maldade.

Se Dom Martinh'é morto, sem prez e sem bondade,
oimais, maos costumes, outro senhor catade,
mais non'o acharedes de Roma atá cidade;
se tal senhor queredes, alhu'lo demandade.

Pero um cavaleiro sei eu, par caridade,
que vos ajudari'a tolher del soidade.
Mais queredes que vos diga ende bem verdade?
Nom é rei nem conde, mais é-x'outra podestade,

que nom direi, que direi, que nom direi . . .

20.

PERO DA PONTE

Song about a Man Who Serves Villainy

This song by Pero da Ponte, dedicated to the infante Don Manuel, begins "Martim Marcos is dead!" and you'll see the connection in the second stanza.

Martim Marcos is dead! God grant it may be!
For if he has died, it's death to dishonesty,
death to folly and death to stupidity,
death to cowardice and death to iniquity.

If Martim has died, then Villainy, be warned,
you'll have to find another lord,
but there's no one like him between here and Rome,
so you'll have to go looking on some other road.

Now I do know of a man, it just so happens,
who could probably cure you of your nostalgia.
Shall I tell you whom I have in mind?
Not a king or count, but from a royal line

that I can't say, I'm saying, can't say . . .

21.

JOAM GARCIA DE GUILHADE

cantiga de amor

Amigos, nom poss'eu negar
a gram coita que d'amor hei,
ca me vejo sandeu andar,
e com sandece o direi:
    os olhos verdes que eu vi
    me fazem ora andar assi.

Pero quem quer x'entenderá
aquestes olhos quaes som,
e dest'alguém se queixará;
mais eu, já quer moira quer nom:
    os olhos verdes que eu vi
    me fazem ora andar assi.

Pero nom devia a perder
home que já o sem nom há
de com sandece rem dizer,
e com sandece dig'eu já:
    os olhos verdes que eu vi
    me fazem ora andar assi.

21.

JOAM GARCIA DE GUILHADE

Song of the Green Eyes

My friends, I can't deny
how badly love has hit me,
because I see how mad I act,
and madly I'll admit it:
    the green eyes I saw
    made me what you see.

It's no secret whose green eyes
I mean, and I know their owner
resents me for alluding to her,
but whether I die or keep on going,
    the green eyes I saw
    made me what you see.

If a man has lost his mind,
he has nothing left to lose
by saying the maddest things,
so I madly say to you:
    the green eyes I saw
    made me what you see.

22.

JOAM GARCIA DE GUILHADE

cantiga de amigo

Vistes, mhas donas, quando noutro dia
o meu amigo conmigo falou,
foi mui queixos', e pero se queixou,
dei-lh'eu entom a cinta que tragia,
mais el demanda-m'or'outra folia.

E vistes (que nunca que m'eu tal visse!),
por s'ir queixar, mias donas, tam sem guisa,
fez-mi tirar a corda da camisa,
e dei-lh'eu dela bem quanta m'el disse,
mais el demanda-mi al—quen'o ferisse!

Sempr'haverá dom Joam de Guilhade,
mentr'el quiser, amigas, das mias dõas,
ca já m'end'el muitas deu e mui bõas;
des i terrei-lhi sempre lealdade,
mais el demanda-m'outra torpidade.

22.

JOAM GARCIA DE GUILHADE

Song about an Insistent Sweetheart

You saw, my gentle ladies, when
my sweetheart came to see me,
how he whined insistently
until I offered him my belt.
Now he's demanding something else.

And you saw, ladies (I wish I hadn't!)
how wildly he kept insisting
until I gave him a piece of string
from my chemise. Now he's demanding
something worthy of a spanking!

Joam de Guilhade is able to obtain
whatever gifts from me he pleases,
since he also gives me lovely presents,
and my loyalty will never wane,
but now he's demanding something insane.

23.

JOAM GARCIA DE GUILHADE

cantiga de amigo

> Amigas, que Deus vos valha, quando veer meu amigo,
> falade sempr'ũas outras enquant'el falar comigo,
> ca muitas cousas diremos
> que ante vós nom diremos.
>
> Sei eu que por falar migo chegará el mui coitado,
> e vós ide-vos chegando lá todas per ess'estrado,
> ca muitas cousas diremos
> que ante vós nom diremos.

23.

JOAM GARCIA DE GUILHADE

Song about a Friend with Things to Say

When my friend comes, girlfriends, please!
talk to each other while he talks to me,
    for we say things to one another
    we'd never say in front of others.

There will be much he longs to say,
so when he comes, stay out of our way,
    for we say things to one another
    we'd never say in front of others.

24.

JOAM GARCIA DE GUILHADE

cantiga de amigo

Cada que vem o meu amig'aqui
diz-m', ai amigas, que perd'o seu sem
por mi, e diz que morre por meu bem,
mais eu bem cuido que nom est assi,
 ca nunca lh'eu vejo morte prender
 nen'o ar vejo nunca ensandecer.

El chora muito e filha-s'a jurar
que é sandeu e quer-me fazer fiz
que por mi morr', e pois morrer nom quis,
mui bem sei eu que há ele vagar,
 ca nunca lh'eu vejo morte prender
 nen'o ar vejo nunca ensandecer.

Ora vejamos o que nos dirá
pois veer viv'e pois sandeu nom for;
ar direi-lh'eu: "Nom morrestes d'amor?"
Mais bem se quite de meu preito já,
 ca nunca lh'eu vejo morte prender
 nen'o ar vejo nunca ensandecer.

E jamais nunca mi fará creer
que por mi morre, ergo se morrer.

24.

JOAM GARCIA DE GUILHADE

Song about a Friend Who Says He Wants to Die

Whenever my friend comes to visit,
he claims to be losing his mind
over me, and he says he's dying
of love, but I'm unconvinced,
    as I have yet to see him dead
    or see him truly lose his head.

He talks in tears about how much
he's out of his mind with love,
and for me (he says) he'd leave
this life, but I guess he's in no rush,
    as I have yet to see him dead
    or see him truly lose his head.

Let's see what he has to say
when next he comes, in perfect health,
and I say, "Hasn't love killed you yet?"
He might as well quit trying to sway me,
    as I have yet to see him dead
    or see him truly lose his head.

I'll never believe he's dying for me
until he dies, truly.

25.

JOAM GARCIA DE GUILHADE

cantiga de amigo

Morr'o meu amigo d'amor
e eu nom vo-lho creo bem,
e el mi diz logo por en
ca verrá morrer u eu for,
    e a mi praz de coraçom
    por veer se morre, se nom.

Enviou-m'el assi dizer:
que eu, por mesura de mim,
o leixasse morrer aqui,
e o veja quando morrer;
    e a mi praz de coraçom
    por veer se morre, se nom.

Mais nunca já crea molher
que por ela morrem assi,
ca nunca eu esse tal vi,
e el moira, se lhi prouguer,
    e a mi praz de coraçom
    por veer se morre, se nom.

25.

JOAM GARCIA DE GUILHADE

Song for a Dying Admirer

My friend is dying of love
for me, but I don't believe it,
and so he says he'll come
and die right at my feet,
    and I would really like to see
    whether or not he dies for me.

He sent a message pleading
with me to be so kind
as to let him die right here
and to watch him while he dies,
    and I would really like to see
    whether or not he dies for me.

Women, don't ever believe
the suitor who would die,
as I have yet to see it,
but if that's his pleasure, fine,
    and I would really like to see
    whether or not he dies for me.

26.

JOAM GARCIA DE GUILHADE

cantiga de amor

Quantos ham gram coita d'amor
eno mundo, qual hoj'eu hei,
querriam morrer, eu o sei,
e haveriam en sabor;
mais mentr'eu vos vir, mia senhor,
    sempre m'eu querria viver
    e atender e atender.

Pero já nom posso guarir,
ca já cegam os olhos meus
por vós, e nom mi val i Deus
nem vós; mais, por vos nom mentir,
enquant'eu vos, mia senhor, vir,
    sempre m'eu querria viver
    e atender e atender.

E tenho que fazem mal sem,
quantos d'amor coitados som,
de querer sa morte, se nom
houverom nunca d'amor bem,
com'eu faç'; e, senhor, por en
    sempre m'eu querria viver
    e atender e atender.

26.

JOAM GARCIA DE GUILHADE

Song of a Lover Who'd Rather Not Die

Many men around the world
who, like me, greatly suffer
from being in love say they'd sooner
die, and no doubt they really would.
But, my lady, while I may see you,
    I'll always want to live
    and keep on waiting!

Even though I can't be cured,
since I see you with blind eyes,
and God does nothing to unbind me,
nor do you, still I'm sure
that while I'm able to see you, lady,
    I'll always want to live
    and keep on waiting!

In my opinion, all of those
who suffer for love and want to die
because, like me, they vainly try
to open a heart forever closed
see it all wrong. Believe me, lady,
    I'll always want to live
    and keep on waiting!

27.

JOAM GARCIA DE GUILHADE

cantiga de amigo

Per boa fé, meu amigo,
mui bem sei eu que m'houvestes
grand'amor e estevestes
mui gram sazom bem comigo,
mais vede-lo que vos digo:
    já safou.

Os grandes nossos amores
que mi e vós sempr'houvemos,
nunca lhi cima fezemos,
coma Brancafrol e Flores,
mais tempo de jogadores
    já safou.

Já eu falei em folia
convosc'e em gram cordura
e em sem e em loucura,
quanto durava o dia,
mais est', ai dom J'am Garcia,
    já safou.

E dessa folia toda
    já safou.

Já safad'é pam de voda,
    já safou.

27.

JOAM GARCIA DE GUILHADE

Song for a Distraught Lover

Indeed, my friend, I know
how much you loved me and
how both of us were happy
to be together, but now
you must accept what's happened:
    it's over.

Although our love was fervent
during the time it lasted,
we didn't act on our passion
like Blanchefleur and Floris,
and now the game of romance
    is over.

I said so many things,
both in and out of my senses,
when crazy or coolheaded,
but those days, Joam Garcia,
are gone, so just accept
    it's over.

That time of craziness
    is over.

The wedding cake that never was
    is over.

28.

JOAM GARCIA DE GUILHADE

cantiga de escárnio

Ai dona fea, fostes-vos queixar
que vos nunca louv'eno meu cantar,
mais ora quero fazer um cantar
em que vos loarei todavia,
e vedes como vos quero loar:
dona fea, velha e sandia!

Dona fea, se Deus mi perdom,
pois havedes atam gram coraçom
que vos eu loe, em esta razom
vos quero já loar todavia,
e vedes qual será a loaçom:
dona fea, velha e sandia!

Dona fea, nunca vos eu loei
em meu trobar, pero muito trobei,
mais ora já um bom cantar farei
em que vos loarei todavia,
e direi-vos como vos loarei:
dona fea, velha e sandia!

28.

JOAM GARCIA DE GUILHADE

Song for an Ugly Lady

Ugly lady, you've complained
that I never sing your praise,
so I've composed a new refrain
    to sing your praise in my own way,
and this is what my song exclaims:
      you're a crazy, old, and ugly lady!

Ugly lady, since your desire
is that I praise you in my rhymes,
God forgive me, I'll now try
    to sing your praise in my own way,
and here's what I, in song, will cry:
      you're a crazy, old, and ugly lady!

Ugly lady, though I've sung
of all my loves, I never sang
a song for you, so now I'll sing,
    singing your praise in my own way,
and this is what my song will say:
      you're a crazy, old, and ugly lady!

29.

JOAM GARCIA DE GUILHADE

cantiga de escárnio

Nunca atam gram torto vi
com'eu prendo d'um infançom,
e quantos ena terra som,
todo'lo têm por assi:
o infançom, cada que quer,
vai-se deitar com sa molher
e nulha rem nom dá por mi.

E já me nunca temerá,
ca sempre me tev'em desdém,
des i ar quer sa molher bem
e já sempr'i filhos fará
—siquer três filhos que fiz i,
filha-os todos pera si:
o Demo lev'o que m'en dá!

Em tam gram coita viv'hoj'eu
que nom poderia maior:
vai-se deitar com mia senhor
e diz do leito que é seu
e deita-se a dormir em paz;
des i, se filh'ou filha faz,
nõn'o quer outorgar por meu!

29.

JOAM GARCIA DE GUILHADE

Song of a Wronged Troubadour

A greater wrong I've never seen
than what this nobleman does to me,
and throughout this region everybody
knows exactly what I mean:
the nobleman, whenever he likes,
goes to bed with his sweet wife
and doesn't pay me any heed.

He'll never fear my competition
but scorn me as he's always done,
and his wife, on whom he dotes,
will always bear him lots of sons;
he even gave his own last name
to the three children that I made
and for my efforts gave me nothing.

My pain's of such a vicious kind
that none could cause me greater dread:
he takes my lady off to bed,
says she's his and spends the night
in peace without a second thought,
and when she bears a son or daughter,
he doesn't recognize it's mine!

30.

JOAM GARCIA DE GUILHADE

cantiga de escárnio

Martim jograr, que gram cousa:
já sempre convosco pousa
   vossa molher!

Veedes m'andar morrendo,
e vós jazedes fodendo
   vossa molher!

Do meu mal nom vos doedes,
e moir'eu, e vós fodedes
   vossa molher!

30.

JOAM GARCIA DE GUILHADE

Song of a Jealous Troubadour

Martin the jongleur, it's not right
that you, not me, hold tight at night
  your wife!

Dying of love, I'm out of luck,
while you, unmoved, lie down to fuck
  your wife!

My suffering matters not to you.
While I die, you screw and screw
  your wife!

31.

ROI QUEIMADO

cantiga de amor

Preguntou Joam Garcia
da morte de que morria,
e dixe-lh'eu todavia:
    —A morte desto xe m'ata:
    Guiomar Afonso Gata
    est a dona que me mata.

Pois que m'houve preguntado
de que era tam coitado,
dixe-lh'eu este recado:
    —A morte desto xe m'ata:
    Guiomar Afonso Gata
    est a dona que me mata.

Dixe-lh'eu: —Já bem vos digo
a coita que hei comigo;
per bõa fé, meu amigo,
    a morte desto xe m'ata:
    Guiomar Afonso Gata
    est a dona que me mata.

31.

Song of the Death I'm Dying

When Joam Garcia inquired
what death it is I'm dying,
this is how I replied:
 "I'm dying a death of passion
 for Guiomar Afonso Gata,
 woman and assassin."

Since he kept on asking
why I was so anguished,
this is what I answered:
 "I'm dying a death of passion
 for Guiomar Afonso Gata,
 woman and assassin."

I said to him, "My friend,
I will indeed explain
the reason for my pain:
 I'm dying a death of passion
 for Guiomar Afonso Gata,
 woman and assassin."

32.

cantiga de amor

Pois que eu ora morto for
sei bem ca dirá mia senhor:
 —Eu sõo Guiomar Afonso!

Pois souber mui bem ca morri
por ela, sei que dirá assi:
 —Eu sõo Guiomar Afonso!

Pois que eu morrer, filhará
entom o soqueix'e dirá:
 —Eu sõo Guiomar Afonso!

32.

ROI QUEIMADO

Song for When I Die

When she learns I've passed away,
this is what my lady will say:
    "Guiomar Afonso is my name!"

When they tell her that I've died,
I know how she will reply:
    "Guiomar Afonso is my name!"

Upon my death, she'll simply place
her chin in palm and then exclaim:
    "Guiomar Afonso is my name!"

33.

PERO GARCIA BURGALÊS

cantiga de escárnio

Roi Queimado morreu com amor
em seus cantares, par Santa Maria,
por ũa dona que gram bem queria;
e por se meter por mais trobador,
porque lh'ela nom quiso bem fazer,
feze-s'el em seus cantares morrer,
mais ressurgiu depois ao tercer dia.

Esto fez el por ũa sa senhor
que quer gram bem, e mais vos en diria:
porque cuida que faz i maestria,
enos cantares que fez há sabor
de morrer i e des i d'ar viver.
Esto faz el, que x'o pode fazer,
mais outr'homem per rem non'o faria.

E nom há já de sa morte pavor,
senom sa morte mais la temeria,
mais sabe bem, per sa sabedoria,
que viverá, des quando morto for,
e faz-s' em seu cantar morte prender,
des i ar vive. Vedes que poder
que lhi Deus deu—mais quen'o cuidaria!

E se mi Deus a mi desse poder
qual hoj'el há, pois morrer, de viver,
jamais eu morte nunca temeria.

33.

PERO GARCIA BURGALÊS

Song about a Troubadour Who Dies and Lives

Roi Queimado died of love
(he swears by heaven) in his verses
because his lady did not love him.
In his effort to convince her
what a fine troubadour he is,
in his songs he passed away
but resurrected on the third day.

He did this for his beloved lady,
a lady he very much adores.
In his songs he tried to show her
that he's a master troubadour
by dying without remaining dead.
Surely no other man on earth
can depart at will, and at will return!

He has no fear of death at all
(were this not so, he'd be less brave),
because he has the practical knowledge
of how to rise up from the grave.
God's hand in this we must acknowledge,
because no other troubadour dies
in the songs he sings and yet survives.

If God gave me that same power
of dying today and living tomorrow,
then death would never make me cower!

34.

cantiga de amor

Se eu a Deus algum mal mereci,
gram vingança soub'El de mim prender,
ca me fez mui bõa dona veer
e mui fremos'e ar fez-me des i
que lhe quis sempre doutra rem melhor.
E pois mi aquesto fez Nostro Senhor,
ar fez ela morrer e leixou-mi

viver no mundo; e mal dia naci
por eu assi eno mundo viver
u Deus sobre mim há tam gram poder
que m'eno mundo faz viver assi
sem ela; ca bem sõo sabedor
d'haver gram coita mentre vivo for,
pois nom vir ela que por meu mal vi!

E por meu mal, amigos, nom morri
u eu primeir'oí dela dizer
que morrera, ca podera perder
vedes qual coita per morrer log'i:
a coita de quantas Deus fez maior,
em que vivo polo seu amor,
pero que nunca bem dela prendi.

110

34.

PERO GARCIA BURGALÊS

Song of a Bereft Lover

If something I did made God take offense,
He exacted on me a cruel revenge
through a woman who in all respects
was beautiful, so that ever since
the day I saw her, nothing else
have I wanted. What Our Lord did next
was to make her die and me persist

in a world like this, where I wish I'd never
been born, since in this world God
has the power to make me go on
and on, living like this, forever
without her. Well do I know I'll suffer
for the rest of my days, yearning to see her,
even though it would have been better

never to have seen a woman so fair.
And better, my friends, if I had died
when I heard the news that she was dead,
because if I'd died, I would have been spared
the worst affliction God ever created:
to live one's life for the love of a lady
who never showed him any favor.

35.

PERO GARCIA BURGALÊS

cantiga de escárnio

Dona Maria Negra, bem talhada,
dizem que sodes de mim namorada.
   Se me bem queredes,
     por Deus, amiga, que m'ôi sorrabedes
   se me bem queredes.

Pois eu tanto por voss'amor hei feito,
ali u vós migo talhastes preito,
   se me bem queredes,
     por Deus, amiga, que m'ôi sorrabedes,
   se me bem queredes.

Por nom viir a mim soa, sinlheira,
venha convosc'a vossa covilheira.
   Se me bem queredes,
     por Deus, amiga, que m'ôi sorrabedes,
   se me bem queredes.

Pois m'eu tanto por vós de peidos vazo,
ali u vós migo talhastes prazo,
   se me bem queredes,
     por Deus, amiga, que m'ôi sorrabedes,
   se me bem queredes.

35.

Song for a Lady in Love with Me

Maria Negra, lady so lovely,
I hear that you're in love with me.
    If you love me, lovely lady,
    all I ask, in the name of God,
    is that you kiss my ass today.

There where you've set up our tryst,
since I've toiled so hard for this,
    if you love me, lovely lady,
    all I ask, in the name of God,
    is that you kiss my ass today.

In order not to journey alone,
why not bring your maid along?
    If you love me, lovely lady,
    all I ask, in the name of God,
    is that you kiss my ass today.

There where you've set up our meeting,
since for you I've long been farting,
    if you love me, lovely lady,
    all I ask, in the name of God,
    is that you kiss my ass today.

36.

PERO GARCIA BURGALÊS

cantiga de escárnio

Maria Negra, desaventuirada!
E por que quer tantas pissas comprar,
pois lhe na mãa nom querem durar
e lh'assi morrem aa malfadada?
E num caralho grande que comprou,
o onte ao serão o esfolou,
e outra pissa tem já amormada.

E já ela é probe tornada,
comprando pissas, vedes que ventuira!
Pissa que compra pouco lhe dura,
sol que a mete na sa pousada,
ca lhi convém que ali moira entom
de polmoeira ou de torcilhom,
ou, per força, fica end'aaguada.

Muit'é pera ventuira menguada,
de tantas pissas no ano perder,
que compra caras, pois lhe vam morrer,
e est'é pola casa molhada
em que as mete, na estrabaria.
E pois lhe morrem, a velha sandia
per pissas será em terra deitada.

114

36.

PERO GARCIA BURGALÊS

Song about a Sad, Impoverished Lady

Maria Negra is looking sadder:
why does she buy so many cocks
when in her hand they always rot,
dying in haste, leaving her shattered?
A big dick purchased yesterday
was by evening completely flayed,
and another cock already has glanders.

She's gotten rather poor in the process
of buying cocks—how sad her lot!
The cocks she buys never last long
after she sticks them in her hospice,
because they always end up dying
of gripes or heaves, or else stop trying,
having worked themselves to exhaustion.

Sadly her funds have been wiped out
from all the cocks she buys in a year:
they cost her dear, then die on her,
and this is because of the damp house
she sticks them in, a smelly stable.
When they die, the crazy old lady
lies there, cockless, on the ground.

37.

PERO GARCIA BURGALÊS

cantiga de escárnio

Que muito mi de Fernam Diaz praz,
que fez el-rei Dom Afonso meirinho,
e nom cata parente nem vezinho
com sabor de tee'la terra em paz:
se o pode por malfeitor saber,
vai sobr'el, e se o pode colher
na mão, logo del justiça faz.

E porque há Dom Fernando gram prez
das gentes todas de mui justiceiro,
o fez el-rei meirinho, dês Viveiro
atá Carriom, ond'outro nunca fez,
e se ouve de malfeitor falar,
vai sobr'el, e nom lhi pod'escapar,
e faz-lhi mal jogo por ũa vez.

E cuidará del quen'o vir aqui,
que o vir andar assi calado,
ca nom sabe parte nem mandado
de tal justiça fazer qual lh'eu vi:
leixou a gente adormecer entom
e trasnoitou sobr'um hom'a Leon,
e fez sobr'el gram justiça log'i.

37.

PERO GARCIA BURGALÊS

Song about a Sheriff Who Deals Out Justice

I'm glad that King Alfonso thought
to make Fernando Diaz sheriff,
as he spares neither friend nor relative
but always keeps the land quite calm:
whenever a wrongdoer comes to his notice
he doesn't rest until getting hold
of the man and really laying it on.

Because Fernando is considered
by everyone to be very fair,
he was made sheriff from Viveiro
to Carrión, where no one ever served,
and if he hears a wrongdoer's near,
he perks right up, going in search
of the man to deal him his just deserts.

Let every visiting man take heed
to keep out of sight, avoiding misdeeds,
for with Fernando you've no idea
of the brutal justice I have seen:
he waited till all were asleep and then
spent the night atop a man in León,
dealing out justice without mercy!

38.

PERO GARCIA BURGALÊS

cantiga de escárnio

Dom Fernando, pero mi maldigades,
quero-vos eu ora desenganar,
ca ouç'as gentes de vós posfaçar
de cavalgar, de que vos nom guardades:
cavalgades pela seest'aqui
e cavalgades de noit'outrossi,
e sospeitam que por mal cavalgades.

Mais rogo-vos ora que mi creades
do que vos ora quero conselhar:
se queredes com as gentes estar,
Dom Fernando, melhor ca nom estades,
sinher, forçade vosso coraçom
e nom cavalguedes tam sem razom,
siquer por vossas bestas, que matades.

38.

PERO GARCIA BURGALÊS

Song to a Man Who Never Stops Mounting

Don Fernando, though you scorn me,
it's as a friend I tell you now
that people are remarking how
your mounting is too rough a sport:
you spend siesta mounting away,
and at night you mount the same,
and they suspect your mounting's sordid.

I beg you now to please consider
how I think this should be handled:
if you desire, Don Fernando,
to live in peace among your kinsmen,
make an effort to curb your passion
and mount less roughly and less rashly.
Think, at least, of the beasts you're killing.

39.

PERO GARCIA BURGALÊS

cantiga de escárnio

Fernand'Escalho vi eu cantar bem,
que poucos outros vi cantar melhor,
e vi-lhe sempre, mentre foi pastor,
mui boa voz, e vi-o cantar bem;
mais ar direi-vos per que o perdeu:
houve sabor de foder, e fodeu,
e perdeu todo o cantar por en.

Nom se guardou de foder, e mal sem
fez el, que nom poderia peor,
e ham-lh'as gentes por en desamor,
per bõa voz que perdeu com mal sem,
voz de cabeça, que xi lhi tolheu,
ca fodeu tanto que lh'enrouqueceu
a voz, e ora já nom canta bem.

E a Dom Fernando conteceu assi:
de mui bõa voz que soía haver
soube-a per avoleza perder,
ca fodeu moç'e nom canta já assi;
ar fodeu pois mui grand'escudeirom,
e ficou ora, se Deus mi perdom,
com a peior voz que nunca oí.

E ora ainda mui grand'infançom
s'i quer foder, que nunca foi sazom
que mais quisesse foder, poilo eu vi.

39.

PERO GARCIA BURGALÊS

Song about a Man Who Once Sang Well

Fernando Escalho once sang well,
as very few have ever sung.
He had, as long as he was young,
a lovely voice that sang quite well,
and now I'll tell you how he lost it:
he liked to fuck and fucked a lot,
so that his singing went to hell.

His fucking got too out of hand,
and nothing could have hurt him more:
people said his singing was poor,
his voice no longer the one he'd had.
He lost the high notes in his voice
from too much fucking—it went hoarse.
And now whatever he sings is bad.

This, in sum, is what occurred:
Don Fernando had a good voice,
which he lost through too much vice;
he fucked a boy and his singing was hurt,
but then he fucked a sizable squire
and, God forgive me, thus acquired
the worst voice I've ever heard.

Now there's another big nobleman
he wants to fuck, and never so much
has he wanted to fuck, from what I've seen.

40.

PERO GARCIA DE AMBROA

cantiga de escárnio

Pedi eu o cono a ũa molher,
e pediu-m'ela cem soldos entom,
e dixe-lh'eu logo: —Mui sem razom
me demandades, mais, se vos prouguer,
fazed'ora—e faredes melhor—
ũa soldada polo meu amor,
a de parte, ca nom hei mais mester.

Fazem soldada do ouro, que val
mui mais ca o vosso cono, de pram;
fazem soldada de vinh'e de pam;
fazem soldada de carn'e de sal.
Por en devedes do cono fazer
soldada, ca nom há-de falescer,
se retalhardes, quem vos compr'o al.

E podede-lo vender, eu o sei,
tod'a retalho, porque saberám
que retalhades, e comprar-vos-am
todos del parte, como eu comprei.
Ainda vos d'al farei mui melhor:
se do embiigo havedes sabor,
contra o rabo vo-lo filharei.

40.

PERO GARCIA DE AMBROA

Song about a Woman Who Charged Too Much

I asked a woman for her cunt,
she quoted me a high price,
and so I said: "It isn't right
to ask a man for that amount.
Now do me and yourself a favor:
sell me a portion of your wares,
as my love won't require much.

"Merchants sell small portions of gold,
worth more than your cunt—don't deny it.
They sell small portions of bread and wine;
for meat and salt, the same thing holds.
Thus you too should sell your cunt,
since other men are sure to come
and buy the portions not yet sold.

"And you'll be able, by this art,
to sell it all, for once word spreads
that you sell piecemeal, many men
like me will gladly buy a part.
I'll even do you a special favor:
if you want to keep your navel,
I'll be happy to take your arse."

41.

PERO MAFALDO

cantiga moral

Devem os ventos andar revolvendo
e mudando aginha os corações
do que põem antre si, ai varões!
e já m'eu aquesto vou aprendendo
e ora cedo mais aprenderei:
a quem poser preito, mentir-lho-ei,
e assi irei melhor guarecendo.

Ca vej'eu ir melhor ao mentireiro
ca o que diz verdade ao seu amigo;
e por aquesto o jur'e o digo
que jamais nunca seja verdadeiro,
mais mentirei e firmarei log'al,
e a quem quero bem, querrei-lhe mal,
e assi guarrei come cavaleiro.

Pois que meu prez nem mia honra nom crece,
porque me quigi teer à verdade,
vêde lo que farei, par caridade,
pois que vej'o que m'assi acaece:
mentirei ao amigo e ao senhor,
e poiará meu prez e meu valor
com mentira, pois com verdade dece.

41.

PERO MAFALDO

Song on How to Win Fame and Honor

The winds, it seems, are overturning
what fickle minds of men—oh men!—
had settled on by common consent,
and now I too am finally learning
(and learning faster every day)
to lie with every oath I make
until at last my luck starts turning.

I see that it's the liar who thrives
rather than the honest friend,
and so I swear never again
to say what's really on my mind.
I'll lie point-blank and that's not all:
those whom I love I'll now defraud,
thereby prospering like a knight.

I've never known much honor or fame
because I've always stuck to truth,
so here is what I'm going to do
to make the situation change:
I'll lie to God and to my friend
so as to boost my honor and fame,
since honesty only made them wane.

42.

NUNO ANES CERZEO

descordo

Agora me quer'eu já espedir
da terra e das gentes que i som,
u mi Deus tanto de pesar mostrou,
e esforçar mui bem meu coraçom
e ar pensar de m'ir alhur guarir,
e a Deus gradesco porque m'en vou.

Ca a meu grad', u m'eu daqui partir,
com seus desejos nom me veeram
chorar, nem ir triste por bem que eu
nunca presesse; nem me poderám
dizer que eu torto faç'em fogir
daqui, u me Deus tanto pesar deu.

Pero das terras haverei soidade,
de que m'or'hei a partir despagado,
e sempr'i tornará o meu cuidado
por quanto bem vi eu en'elas já;
ca já por al nunca me veerá
nulh'home ir triste nem desconortado.

E bem dig'a Deus, pois m'en vou, verdade:
se eu das gentes algum sabor havia,
ou das terras em que eu guarecia,
por aquest'era tod'e nom por al,
mais ora já nunca me será mal
de me partir delas e m'ir mia via.

. . .

42.

NUNO ANES CERZEO

Discord

All I want is to take my leave
of these people and this land
where God has shown me so much grief.
I'll do my best not to lose morale,
I'll start again, take up a new life
somewhere else. Thank God I can.

Once I've willingly, gladly left,
I'll never be homesick for this place
nor waste any tears recollecting
the good times God never granted me.
No one who knows the sorrow I've felt
can think it was wrong of me to flee.

And yet I'll miss, in a way, the land
I'm about to leave, disenchanted:
my thoughts will constantly return
to whatever love I had there.
But that will be the only reason
I may, at times, have a sad air.

Since I'm going, I'll tell God the truth:
any affection I might have felt
for these people and this land
was only due to that love I happened
to experience. I'll be a happier man
once this place is in my past.

. . .

Ca sei de mi
quanto sofri
e encobri
en'esta terra de pesar.
Como perdi
e despendi,
vivend'aqui,
meus dias, posso-m'en queixar.

E cuidarei
e pensarei
quant'aguardei
o bem que nunca pud'achar.
E forçar-m'-ei
e prenderei,
como guarrei,
conselh'agor' a meu cuidar.

Pensar
d'achar
logar
provar
quer'eu veer se poderei;
o sem
d'alguém
ou rem
de bem
me valha, se o em mi hei.

. . .

Well I know
how much I sighed
and held inside
in this land of pain;
the things I missed,
the time I lost
by staying on:
I've good cause to complain.

I'll remember
with regret
how I waited
for the good I couldn't find,
and I'll attempt
step by step
to at least attain
a peaceful state of mind.

I'd like
to try
to find
a kindly
place in which to live.
May a friend's
good sense
or some good
(if there's good)
in myself help me thrive.

. . .

Valer,
poder
saber
dizer,
bem me possa, que eu d'ir hei;
d'haver
poder
prazer
prender
poss'eu, pois esto cobrarei.

Assi
querrei
buscar
viver
outra vida, que provarei,
e meu descord' acabarei.

May wisdom
my will
and words
uphold me
now that I must go.
God grant
that I
might find
the pleasure
I've yet to know.

Yes I
would like
to try
to live
a life completely new,
and my discord thus conclude.

43.

JOAM SOARES COELHO

cantiga de amigo

Fui eu, madre, lavar meus cabelos
a la fonte e paguei-m'eu delos
  e de mi, louçana.

Fui eu, madre, lavar mias garcetas
a la fonte e paguei-m'eu delas
  e de mi, louçana.

A la fonte e paguei-m'eu deles;
aló achei, madr', o senhor deles
  e de mi, louçana.

E ante que m'eu d'ali partisse
fui pagada do que m'ele disse
  e de mi, louçana.

43.

JOAM SOARES COELHO

Song of the Beautiful Hair

Mother, I went to the spring
to wash my hair and found it pretty
and my own self fair.

Mother, I went to the pool
to wash my hair and found it beautiful
and my own self fair.

Washing my hair I found it beautiful
and met, at the pool, the man who rules it
and my own self, fair.

Before I took my leave of him
I found the words he told me pleasing
and my own self fair.

44.

FERNÃO GARCIA ESGARAVUNHA

cantiga de escárnio

Esta ama, cuj'é Joam Coelho,
per bõas manhas que soub'aprender,
cada u for, achará bom conselho:
ca sabe bem fiar e bem tecer
e talha mui bem bragas e camisa,
e nunca vistes molher de sa guisa
que mais límpia vida sábia fazer.

Ante, hoj'é das molheres preçadas
que nós sabemos em nosso logar,
ca lava bem e faz bõas queijadas
e sabe bem moer e amassar
e sabe muito de bõa leiteira.
Esto nom dig'eu por bem que lhi queira,
mais porque est assi, a meu cuidar.

E seu marido, de crastar verrões
nom lh'acham par, de Burgos a Carrion,
nem a ela de capar galiões
fremosament', assi Deus mi perdom.
Tod'esto faz, e cata bem argueiro
e escanta bem per olh'e per calheiro
e sabe muito bõa escantaçom.

. . .

44.

FERNÃO GARCIA ESGARAVUNHA

Song in Praise of a Nursemaid Lady

The nursemaid lady of Joam Coelho
knows so many practical things
that she's a godsend wherever she goes:
she's just great at sewing and weaving,
making the loveliest shirts and pants,
and you've never seen a girl of her class
lead a life more wholesome and clean.

Around these parts I must confess
she's one of the finest women we know:
good at washing, baking cakes,
grinding flour, and kneading dough,
and she's also a marvelous milkmaid.
I don't say this as a favor
but because I really think it's so.

For castrating pigs, her husband excels
like no one else from Burgos to Carrión,
while only she, God save me, slices
off rooster balls with such loving care.
And that's not all: she can read signs,
can skillfully cast an evil eye,
and is well versed in magic cures.

. . .

Nom acharedes em toda Castela,
graças a Deus, de que mi agora praz,
melhor ventrulho nem melhor morcela
do que a ama com sa mão faz.
E al faz bem, como diz seu marido:
faz bom souriç'e lava bem transido
e deita bem galinha choca assaz.

You won't find in the whole of Castile
(bless her for making my tummy happy!)
sausage or blood pudding that compares
to what you'll get from this maid's hand.
And besides all that, her husband reports
she makes fine tripe, can wash a corpse,
and knows how to get any egg to hatch.

45.

JUIÃO BOLSEIRO

cantiga de amigo

Fez ũa cantiga d'amor
ora meu amigo por mi,
que nunca melhor feita vi,
mais, como x'é mui trobador,
fez ũas lirias no som
que mi sacam o coraçom.

Muito bem se soube buscar
por mi ali, quando a fez,
em loar-mi muit'e meu prez,
mais, de pram, por xe mi matar,
fez ũas lirias no som
que mi sacam o coraçom.

Per bõa fé, bem baratou
de a por mi bõa fazer,
e muito lho sei gradecer,
mais vedes de que me matou:
fez ũas lirias no som
que mi sacam o coraçom.

45.

JUIÃO BOLSEIRO

Song about a Song of Love

I've never heard a lovelier
song than the one my beloved
made for me and, being
the gifted troubadour he is,
    he wrote a musical part
    that slew my heart.

My beloved knew how to make
an endearing song by praising
me and my best qualities,
and he knew how to kill me
    with a musical part
    that slew my heart.

He sang the perfect words
to make me look most worthy,
which naturally pleased me,
but what really killed me
    was a musical part
    that slew my heart.

46.

JUIÃO BOLSEIRO

cantiga de amigo

Sem meu amigo manh'eu senlheira,
e sol nom dormem estes olhos meus,
e quant'eu posso peç'a luz a Deus
e nom mi a dá, per nulha maneira.
    Mais se masesse com meu amigo,
    a luz agora seria migo.

Quand'eu com meu amigo dormia,
a noite nom durava nulha rem,
e ora dur'a noit'e vai e vem,
nom vem a luz nem parec'o dia.
    Mais se masesse com meu amigo,
    a luz agora seria migo.

E segundo com'a mi parece,
u migo mam meu lum'e meu senhor,
vem log'a luz, de que nom hei sabor,
e ora vai noit'e vem e crece.
    Mais se masesse com meu amigo,
    a luz agora seria migo.

Pater Nostrus rez'eu mais de cento
por Aquel que morreu na vera cruz,
que el mi mostre mui cedo a luz,
mais mostra-mi as noites d'Avento.
    Mais se masesse com meu amigo,
    a luz agora seria migo.

46.

JUIÃO BOLSEIRO

Song on an Unending Night

I get so lonely without my lover
even my eyes are unable to rest:
I pray for light with every breath,
but God refuses me this favor.
 If with my lover I'd spent the night,
 it would already be light.

When my lover and I slept together,
before I knew it the night was gone,
but now the night goes on and on:
the light of the new day takes forever.
 If with my lover I'd spent the night,
 it would already be light.

Yes, I have the distinct impression
that when my lord and flame is with me
the light breaks almost immediately,
chasing away our night of passion.
 If with my lover I'd spent the night,
 it would already be light.

Sometimes I say a hundred Our Fathers
for the One who died on the true cross,
in hopes the day will soon dawn,
but Advent nights are all He offers.
 If with my lover I'd spent the night,
 it would already be light.

47.

JUIÃO BOLSEIRO

cantiga de amigo

Aquestas noites tam longas que
Deus fez em grave dia
por mim, por que as nom dórmio,
e por que as nom fazia
    no tempo que meu amigo
    soía falar comigo?

Porque as fez Deus tam grandes,
nom posso eu dormir, coitada,
e, de como som sobejas,
quisera-m'outra vegada
    no tempo que meu amigo
    soía falar comigo.

Porque as Deus fez tam grandes,
sem mesura, desiguaes,
e as eu dormir nom posso,
por que as nom fez ataes
    no tempo que meu amigo
    soía falar comigo?

47.

JUIÃO BOLSEIRO

Song of the Long Nights God Made

These terribly long nights
God made on a day unhappy
for me, who cannot sleep!
Why weren't they long lasting
    when my beloved, after dark,
    used to come by and talk?

Why did God make them so long,
and me so sleepless and bored?
If only the nights had been
so endlessly long before
    when my beloved, after dark,
    used to come by and talk!

Why did God make them so long,
these nights that never cease,
when I can't sleep? Why didn't
He make nights like these
    when my beloved, after dark,
    used to come by and talk?

48.

PEDRO ANES SOLAZ

cantiga de amigo

Eu velida nom dormia
    lelia doura
e meu amigo venia
    edoi lelia doura.

Nom dormia e cuidava
    lelia doura
e meu amigo chegava
    edoi lelia doura.

O meu amigo venia
    lelia doura
e d'amor tam bem dizia
    edoi lelia doura.

O meu amigo chegava
    lelia doura
e d'amor tam bem cantava
    edoi lelia doura.

Muito desejei, amigo,
    lelia doura
que vos tevesse comigo
    edoi lelia doura.

Muito desejei, amado,
    lelia doura
que vos tevess'a meu lado
    edoi lelia doura.

. . .

48.

PEDRO ANES SOLAZ

Song for a Sleepless Night

Lovely and wide awake
    it's my turn
with my friend on his way
    today it's my turn.

Awake the whole night
    it's my turn
till at last he arrives
    today it's my turn.

My friend on his way
    it's my turn
with sweet nothings to say
    today it's my turn.

When at last he arrives
    it's my turn
how sweet are his rhymes
    today it's my turn.

How long I've been wishing
    it's my turn
to have you here with me
    today it's my turn.

How long I've desired
    it's my turn
to have you at my side
    today it's my turn.

Leli, leli, par Deus, leli
  lelia doura
bem sei eu quem nom diz leli
  edoi lelia doura.

Bem sei eu quem nom diz leli
  lelia doura
demo x'é quem nom diz leli
  edoi lelia doura.

It's my night, by God, my night
    it's my turn
I know who won't say "my night"
    today it's my turn.

I know who won't say "my night"
    it's my turn
That witch won't say "my night"
    today it's my turn.

49.

JOAM LOPES DE ULHOA

cantiga de amor

A mia senhor, que me foi amostrar
Deus por meu mal, por vos eu nom mentir,
e que sempr'eu punhei de a servir
muit', houve gram sabor de m'enganar:
ca me falou primeir', u a vi, bem,
e pois que viu que perdia o sem
por ela, nunca m'er quiso falar.

E se m'eu dela soubesse guardar,
quando a vi, punhara de guarir,
mais foi-m'ela bem falar e riir,
e falei-lh'eu, e nom a vi queixar,
nem se queixou que a chamei "senhor".
E pois me viu mui coitado d'amor,
prougo-lhe muit'e nom m'er quis catar!

E pois me queria desemparar,
quando a vi, mandasse-me partir
logo de si, e mandasse-m'end'ir.
Mais nom lhe vi de nulha rem pesar
que lh'eu dissesse, tam bem me catou!
E pois viu que seu amor me forçou,
leixou-m'assi desemparad'andar.

. . .

49.

JOAM LOPES DE ULHOA

Song about a Two-Faced Lady

My lady, through whom God ordained
(if truth be told) my present misery,
a lady I did my best to serve,
was pleased to mock me with disdain.
At first she talked to me with fervor,
but once she saw I was mad for her,
she never talked to me again.

The day we met, had I thought to remain
aloof, I would have avoided much suffering,
but she started to talk and laughed freely,
so I talked too—she didn't complain;
she didn't protest when I called her "lady."
But on seeing how much my heart was aching,
she found it amusing—and sent me away!

If she wanted to get rid of me,
she should have told me, when we met,
to disappear that very moment.
But when I talked, she didn't seem
to mind, and looked upon me fondly!
Once she saw my heart was conquered,
she dropped me without a shred of pity.

. . .

E deferença dev'end'a filhar
tod'home, que dona fremosa vir,
de mim: e guarde-se bem de nom ir,
com'eu fui log', em seu poder entrar,
ca lh'averrá com'aveo a mim:
servi-a muit', e pois que a servi,
fez-mi aquesto quant'oídes contar!

Every man who meets a special
lady should learn from my experience,
and take good care to keep his distance,
never falling under her spell,
lest he suffer the same fate as me:
after faithfully serving my lady,
she did just what you've heard me tell!

50.

GIL PERES CONDE

cantiga de amor

Já eu nom hei por quem trobar
e já nom hei en coraçom,
porque nom hei já quem amar;
por en mi míngua razom,
ca mi filhou Deus mia senhor.
Ah, que filh'o Demo maior
quantas cousas que suas som,

como lh'outra vez já filhou
a cadeira u siia
o Filh'! E porque mi filhou
bõa senhor que havia?
E diz El que nom há molher.
Se a nom há, pera que quer
pois tant'à bõa Maria?

Deus nunca mi a mi nada deu
e tolhe-me bõa senhor.
Por esto nom creo en'El eu
nem me tenh'en por pecador,
ca me fez mia senhor perder.
Catade que mi foi fazer,
confiand'eu no seu amor!

. . .

152

50.

GIL PERES CONDE

Song against God for Taking My Lady

I've lost whatever longing
I had to make troubadour songs,
because I have no one to love.
My inspiration was robbed
from me when God took away
my lady. So the devil take
whatever belongs to God,

as he took, in a former age,
the chair where the Son sat!
Why did God have to take
the good lady I once had?
He says He has no lady,
but why then to blessed Mary
is He so closely attached?

God never gave me a thing,
and He carried off my good lady.
That's why I don't believe
in Him or my sins. The blame
for my lady's loss was His.
Look at what God did
to one who relied on His grace!

. . .

Nunca se Deus mig'averrá
se mi nom der mia senhora;
mais como mi o corregerá?
Destroia-m', ante ca morra.
Hom'é: tod'aqueste mal faz,
como fez já o gram malvaz,
em Sodoma e Gomorra.

I'll never make up with God
till He gives me back my lady,
but what He'll do instead
is torture me till I die.
He's a man: all the horror
of Sodom and Gomorrah
He wreaks on me today.

51.

GIL PERES CONDE

cantiga de escárnio

> Pôs conta el-rei em todas sas fronteiras
> que nem em vilas nem em carreiras
>   que nom cômiam galinhas na guerra,
> ca diz que dizem as veedeiras
>   que será perdimento da terra.
>
> A concelhos e a cavaleiros
> mandam comer vacas e carneiros,
>   mais nom cômiam galinhas na guerra,
> ca diz que dizem os aguireiros
>   que será perdimento da terra.
>
> Cômiam porcos frescos e toucinhos,
> cabritos, cachaç'e ansarinhos,
>   mais nom cômiam galinhas na guerra,
> ca diz que lhi dizem os devinhos
>   que será perdimento da terra.

51.

GIL PERES CONDE

Song about What Not to Eat in War

The king sent orders to all the borders
—both in the towns and along the way—
    that no one at war eat chicken meat,
because he says the diviners say
    that this would mean a sure defeat.

He told the townships and his knights
to eat all the lamb and beef they want
    but not, during war, any chicken meat,
because he says the soothsayers warn
    that this would mean a sure defeat.

Let them eat roast pig and bacon,
salted pork head, geese and goat,
    but not, while at war, any chicken meat,
because he says the seers note
    that this would mean a sure defeat.

52.

GIL PERES CONDE

cantiga de escárnio

Os vossos meus maravedis, senhor,
que eu nom houvi, que servi melhor
ou tam bem come outr'a que os dam,
hei os d'haver enquant'eu vivo for,
ou à mia mort', ou quando mi os darám?

A vossa mia soldada, senhor Rei,
que eu servi e serv'e servirei,
com'outro quem quer a que a dam bem,
hei a d'haver enquant'a viver hei,
ou à mia mort', ou que mi farám en?

Os vossos meus dinheiros, senhor, nom
pud'eu haver, pero servidos som,
come outros, que os ham de servir;
hei os d'haver mentr'eu viver, ou pom-
-mi-os à mia mort', ou a quem os vou pedir?

Ca passou temp'e trastempados som,
houve an'e dia e quero-m'en partir.

52.

GIL PERES CONDE

Song of an Unpaid Soldier

Thy my money, good sir,
which I haven't received, though I served
like others who've already been paid—
will I get it while I'm alive on earth
or after I'm already dead?

Thy my wages, good king,
whom I served, serve, and will serve,
like anyone paid for his work—
will I get them while still living
or only after I've left this world?

Thy my salary, good lord,
for service I duly performed,
while others have yet to do theirs—
will you pay it to me before
I die, or when I'm no longer here?

For it's long overdue,
it's been a year and a day,
and I'd like to be on my way.

53.

AFONSO MENDES DE BESTEIROS

cantiga de escárnio

Dom Foão, que eu sei que há preço de livão,
vedes que fez ena guerra—daquesto são certão:
sol que viu os genetes, come boi que fer tavão,
  sacudiu-se e revolveu-se, al-
  çou rab'e foi sa via a Portugal.

Dom Foão, que eu sei que há preço de ligeiro,
vedes que fez ena guerra—daquesto som verdadeiro:
sol que viu os genetes, come bezerro tenreiro,
  sacudiu-se e revolveu-se, al-
  çou rab'e foi sa via a Portugal.

Dom Foão, que eu sei que há prez de liveldade,
vedes que fez ena guerra—sabede-o por verdade:
sol que viu os genetes, come cam que sal de grade,
  sacudiu-se e revolveu-se, al-
  çou rab'e foi sa via a Portugal.

53.

AFONSO MENDES DE BESTEIROS

Song about a Nobleman Sent to Fight the Moors

Sir You-Know-Who is known to get rattled.
All I know is how he acted in battle:
seeing the cavalry, like a bull when stabbed
    he shook his fur, turned in his tracks,
    lifted his tail, and hied straight back
    to Portugal.

Sir You-Know-Who is known to panic.
All I know is how he acted in combat:
seeing the cavalry, like a heifer calf
    he shook his fur, turned in his tracks,
    lifted his tail, and hied straight back
    to Portugal.

Sir You-Know-Who is known as a weakling.
All I know is what he did on the field:
seeing the cavalry, like a dog unleashed
    he shook his fur, turned in his tracks,
    lifted his tail, and hied straight back
    to Portugal.

54.

ALFONSO X, KING OF CASTILE AND LEÓN

cantiga moral

Nom me posso pagar tanto
do canto
das aves nem de seu som
nem d'amor nem de missom
nem d'armas—ca hei espanto
por quanto
mui perigoosas som
—come d'um bom galeom
que mi alongue muit'aginha
deste demo da campinha,
u os alacrães som;
ca dentro, no coraçom,
senti deles a espinha.

E juro par Deus lo santo
que manto
nom tragerei, nem granhom,
nem terrei d'amor razom,
nem d'armas, porque quebranto
e chanto
vem delas tod'a sazom;
mais tragerei um dormom,
e irei pela marinha
vendend'azeite e farinha,
e fugirei do poçom
do alacrã, ca eu nom
lhi sei outra meezinha.

. . .

54.

ALFONSO X, KING OF CASTILE AND LEÓN

Song of a Man Weary of Scorpions

No longer can I be cheered
by the chirping
and delicate songs of birds,
nor by love or work,
nor by weapons (whose perils,
I confess,
make me almost tremble),
but only by a good vessel
to take me with all due speed
away from this land's demon
heart, full of scorpions,
as my heart knows, stung
by the bite of their poison.

I swear by Holy God
I'll go
without a beard or a cloak,
keeping my heart closed
to love and taking no weapons
(which always
lead to grief and disaster):
a boat is all I ask for.
With it I will sail
along the coast, selling
oil and flour, fleeing
(I know no other remedy)
from the scorpions' sting.

...

Nem de lançar a tavolado
pagado
nom sõo, se Deus m'ampar,
adés, nem de bafordar,
e andar de noute armado,
sem grado
o faço, e a roldar,
ca mais me pago do mar
que de seer cavaleiro;
ca eu foi já marinheiro
e quero-m'oimais guardar
do alacrã, e tornar
ao que me foi primeiro.

E direi-vos um recado:
pecado
já me nom pod'enganar
que me faça já falar
em armas, ca nom m'é dado
(doado
m'é de as eu razõar,
poilas nom hei a provar);
ante quer'andar sinlheiro
e ir come mercadeiro
algũa terra buscar
u me nom possam culpar
alacrã negro nem veiro.

I'm not fond of tilting
at targets,
nor do I find jousting
(God forgive me) enjoyable,
and to spend my nights in armor
on rounds
isn't at all appealing:
I'd rather be a seaman
than keep on as a knight.
When I was young I plied
the waters, and I've decided
to take up that old life
and leave scorpions behind.

I still have this to tell:
the devil
will never be able to fool me
into talking about using
weapons, which aren't for me
(indeed
it's useless to mention weapons,
as I'm certain not to wear them).
I'd rather sail, alone,
as a simple merchantman,
until I find a land
where I know I can't be stung
by black or spotted scorpions.

55.

ALFONSO X, KING OF CASTILE AND LEÓN

cantiga de Santa Maria

ESTA É DE LOOR DE SANTA MARIA, COM' É FREMOSA E
BÕA E Á GRAN PODER.

Rosa das rosas e Fror das frores,
Dona das donas, Sennor das sennores.

Rosa de beldad' e de parecer
e Fror d'alegria e de prazer,
Dona en mui piadosa seer,
Sennor en toller coitas e doores.
Rosa das rosas e Fror das frores,
Dona das donas, Sennor das sennores.

Atal Sennor dev' ome muit' amar,
que de todo mal o pode guardar;
e pode-ll' os peccados perdõar,
que faz no mundo per maos sabores.
Rosa das rosas e Fror das frores,
Dona das donas, Sennor das sennores.

Devemo-la muit' amar e servir,
ca punna de nos guardar de falir;
des i dos erros nos faz repentir,
que nos fazemos come pecadores.
Rosa das rosas e Fror das frores,
Dona das donas, Sennor das sennores.

. . .

55.

ALFONSO X, KING OF CASTILE AND LEÓN

Song in Praise of Holy Mary

**THIS IS IN PRAISE OF HOLY MARY, TELLING HOW SHE IS
LOVELY AND GOOD AND DOES GREAT THINGS.**

Woman among women, Lady of ladies,
Rose among roses, Flower of flowers.

Rose of beauty and gracefulness,
Flower fresh and full of bliss,
Woman who always comforts us,
Lady who takes away all sorrows.
Woman among women, Lady of ladies,
Rose among roses, Flower of flowers.

Every man should greatly love
the Lady who keeps us safe from evil
and, when we're weak, is merciful,
forgiving whatever sins be ours.
Woman among women, Lady of ladies,
Rose among roses, Flower of flowers.

We should greatly love and serve her,
since from evil she preserves us,
and if we sin, she can turn us
away from the errors of our dark hours.
Woman among women, Lady of ladies,
Rose among roses, Flower of flowers.

. . .

Esta dona que tenno por Sennor
e de que quero seer trobador,
se eu per ren poss' aver seu amor,
dou ao Demo os outros amores.
    Rosa das rosas e Fror das frores,
    Dona das donas, Sennor das sennores.

If this Virgin I take for my Lady
and praise in song as a troubadour
will give me her love, I'll surrender
my other loves to the evil powers.
Woman among women, Lady of ladies,
Rose among roses, Flower of flowers.

56.

ALFONSO X, KING OF CASTILE AND LEÓN

cantiga de Santa Maria

**ESTA É DE LOOR DE SANTA MARIA, DO
DEPARTIMENTO QUE Á ENTRE AVE E EVA.**

Entre Av' e Eva
gran departiment' á.

Ca Eva nos tolleu
o Parays' e Deus,
Ave nos y meteu;
porend', amigos meus:
 Entre Av' e Eva
 gran departiment' á.

Eva nos foi deitar
do dem' en sa prijon,
e Ave en sacar;
e por esta razon:
 Entre Av' e Eva
 gran departiment' á.

Eva nos fez perder
amor de Deus e ben,
e pois Ave aver
no-lo fez; e poren:
 Entre Av' e Eva
 gran departiment' á.

. . .

56.

ALFONSO X, KING OF CASTILE AND LEÓN
Song in Praise of Holy Mary

**THIS IS IN PRAISE OF HOLY MARY, TELLING THE
DIFFERENCE BETWEEN AVE AND EVE.**

> *Don't be deceived:*
> *Ave isn't Eve!*

Through Eve we forfeited
God and his heaven,
but Ave restored them,
and so, my friends,
   don't be deceived:
   Ave isn't Eve!

It was Eve who threw us
into Satan's prison
but Ave withdrew us,
and so, for this reason,
   don't be deceived:
   Ave isn't Eve!

Through Eve we lost
God's love and grace;
through Ave we got
them back. And thus—
   don't be deceived:
   Ave isn't Eve!

. . .

Eva nos ensserrou
os çeos sen chave,
e Maria britou
as portas per Ave.
　　Entre Av' e Eva
　　gran departiment' á.

It was Eve who bolted
shut the heavens
and Mary who opened
their doors through Ave.
Don't be deceived:
Ave isn't Eve!

57.

ALFONSO X, KING OF CASTILE AND LEÓN

cantiga de Santa Maria

COMO SANTA MARIA FEZE ESTAR O MONGE TREZENTOS
ANOS AO CANTO DA PASSARŸA, PORQUE LLE PEDIA QUE
LLE MOSTRASSE QUAL ERA O BEN QUE AVIAN OS QUE
ERAN EN PARAISO.

     Quena Virgen ben servirá
     a Parayso irá.

E daquest' un gran miragre vos quer' eu ora contar,
que fezo Santa Maria por un monge, que rogar
ll'ia sempre que lle mostrasse qual ben en Parais' á
     Quena Virgen ben servirá
     a Parayso irá.

E que o viss' en ssa vida ante que fosse morrer.
E porend' a Groriosa vedes que lle foi fazer:
fez-lo entrar en hũa orta en que muitas vezes ja
     Quena Virgen ben servirá
     a Parayso irá.

Entrara; mais aquel dia fez que hũa font' achou
mui crara e mui fremosa, e cab' ela s'assentou.
E pois lavou mui ben sas mãos, diss': "Ai, Virgen, que será
     Quena Virgen ben servirá
     a Parayso irá.

     . . .

174

57.

ALFONSO X, KING OF CASTILE AND LEÓN

Song of a Miracle by Holy Mary

HOW HOLY MARY MADE A MONK SIT STILL FOR THREE
HUNDRED YEARS, ENCHANTED BY A BIRD'S SINGING, BE-
CAUSE HE HAD ASKED TO BE SHOWN THE WONDERS EN-
JOYED BY THOSE IN HEAVEN.

> *Who serves the Virgin well*
> *will in heaven dwell.*

Concerning this refrain I'll tell a miraculous deed
performed by Holy Mary because of a monk who pleaded
to be shown by her what kind of wonders heaven held
> *Who serves the Virgin well*
> *will in heaven dwell.*

and to be shown them in this life, before he died.
Now see what our Glorious Lady therefore did:
she made him enter a garden where he often went,
> *Who serves the Virgin well*
> *will in heaven dwell.*

but on that day she made him find a beautiful fountain
with clear water, next to which the monk sat down.
And after washing his hands he said, "Virgin, tell me,
> *Who serves the Virgin well*
> *will in heaven dwell.*

. . .

Se verei do Parayso, o que ch' eu muito pidi,
algun pouco de seu viço ante que saya daqui,
e que sábia do que ben obra que galardon averá?"
    Quena Virgen ben servirá
    a Parayso irá.

Tan toste que acabada ouv' o mong' a oraçon,
oyu hūa passarinna cantar log' en tan bon son,
que sse escaeceu seendo e catando sempr' alá.
    Quena Virgen ben servirá
    a Parayso irá.

Atan gran sabor avia daquel cant' e daquel lais,
que grandes trezentos anos estevo assi, ou mays,
cuidando que non estevera senon pouco, com' está
    Quena Virgen ben servirá
    a Parayso irá.

Mong' algūa vez no ano, quando sal ao vergeu.
Des i foi-ss' a passarynna, de que foi a el mui greu,
e diz: "Eu daqui ir-me quero, ca oy mais comer querrá
    Quena Virgen ben servirá
    a Parayso irá.

O convent'." E foi-sse logo e achou un gran portal
que nunca vira, e disse: "Ai, Santa Maria, val!
Non é est' o meu mõesteiro, pois de mi que se fará?"
    Quena Virgen ben servirá
    a Parayso irá.

. . .

may I now see heaven, and something of its pleasures
(as I've so often asked) before I leave this place?
And may I see the prize of those who follow the Way?"
Who serves the Virgin well
will in heaven dwell.

No sooner had the monk concluded his earnest prayer
than he heard a bird singing such a beautiful air
he forgot himself and stared into space as if in a spell.
Who serves the Virgin well
will in heaven dwell.

So very pleasant was the singing in his ears
that he stayed there for three hundred or more years,
thinking he hadn't stayed but a short while, as when
Who serves the Virgin well
will in heaven dwell.

a monk, every now and then, spends time in the garden.
Once the bird had left, the monk felt downhearted
and said, "I'd better go. The convent must be waiting
Who serves the Virgin well
will in heaven dwell.

for me to eat." And so he went and found another
portal than what he knew, and said, "Blessed Mother,
this is not my monastery. May God help me!"
Who serves the Virgin well
will in heaven dwell.

. . .

Des i entrou na eigreja, e ouveron gran pavor
os monges quando o viron, e demandou-ll' o prior,
dizend': "Amigo, vos quen sodes ou que buscades acá?"
  Quena Virgen ben servirá
  a Parayso irá.

Diss' el: "Busco meu abade, que agor' aqui leixey,
e o prior e os frades, de que mi agora quitey
quando fui a aquela orta; u seen quen mio dirá?"
  Quena Virgen ben servirá
  a Parayso irá.

Quand' est' oyu o abade, teve-o por de mal sen,
e outrossi o convento; mais des que souberon ben
de como fora este feyto, disseron: "Quen oyrá
  Quena Virgen ben servirá
  a Parayso irá.

Nunca tan gran maravilla como Deus por este fez
polo rogo de ssa Madre, Virgen santa de gran prez!
E por aquesto a loemos; mais quena non loará
  Quena Virgen ben servirá
  a Parayso irá.

Mais d'outra cousa que seja? Ca, par Deus, gran dereit' é,
pois quanto nos lle pedimos nos dá seu Fill', a la ffe,
por ela, e aqui nos mostra o que nos depois dará."
  Quena Virgen ben servirá
  a Parayso irá.

Then he entered the church, frightening all the friars
with his strange appearance, until at last the prior
asked, "Who are you and what do you seek, my friend?"
  Who serves the Virgin well
  will in heaven dwell.

He answered, "I seek my abbot, who was here just now,
and the prior and friars I left behind when I went down
to the garden: can you tell me where they went?"
  Who serves the Virgin well
  will in heaven dwell.

Hearing this, the abbot judged the monk insane,
and so did the entire convent, but once it was explained
exactly what had happened, then they all exclaimed:
  Who serves the Virgin well
  will in heaven dwell.

"Never was God known to do a more marvelous work
at the request of his Mother, the Virgin so very worthy.
For this we praise her, and who wouldn't, above all else,
  Who serves the Virgin well
  will in heaven dwell.

offer her their praise? God knows, it's only right,
since all we ask is granted by her son, the Christ,
at her urging, and here she shows us our future wealth."
  Who serves the Virgin well
  will in heaven dwell.

58.

ALFONSO X, KING OF CASTILE AND LEÓN

cantiga de escárnio

Ao daiam de Cález eu achei
livros que lhe levavam de Berger,
e o que os tragia preguntei
por eles, e respondeu-m'el: —Senher,
com estes livros que vós vedes, dous,
e con'os outros que el tem dos sous,
fod'el per eles quanto foder quer.

E ainda vos end'eu mais direi:
macar ena Lei muit'haja mester
leer, por quant'eu sa fazenda sei,
con'os livros que tem, nom há molher
a que nom faça que semelhem grous
os corvos e as anguias babous,
per força de foder, se x'el quiser.

Ca nom há mais, na arte do foder,
do que enos livros que el tem jaz;
e el há tal sabor de os leer
que nunca noite nem dia al faz;
e sabe d'arte do foder tam bem
que, con'os seus livros d'artes que el tem,
fod'el as mouras, cada que lhi praz.

E mais vos contarei de seu saber
que cõn'os livros que el tem i faz:
manda-os ante si todos trager,
e pois que fode per eles assaz,

. . .

58.

ALFONSO X, KING OF CASTILE AND LEÓN

Song about the Dean's Books

I met a man carrying books
from Berger to Cádiz's dean,
and when I asked to take a look,
he said, "Sir, the two books you see
and others the dean has just like these
allow him to fuck as much as he pleases.

"And that's not all: in spite of having
to read and study canon law,
with books like these the dean of Cádiz
puts the women he fucks in thrall,
so much so that they end up seeing
cranes as crows, and silkworms as eels.

"When it comes to the art of fucking,
his books have all you need to know,
and he does absolutely nothing
but read them day and night, and so
when it comes to fucking he's a master
and fucks every Moorish dame he's after.

"There are things that he can do
with his books like no one else:
he leaves them open while he screws,
and should some woman be possessed,
he fucks her with such skill and art
the evil demon soon departs.

. . .

se molher acha que o demo tem,
assi a fode per arte e per sem,
que saca dela o demo malvaz.

E com tod'esto, ainda faz al
con'os livros que tem, per bõa fé:
se acha molher que haja o mal
deste fogo que de Sam Marçal é,
assi a vai per foder encantar
que, fodendo, lhi faz bem semelhar
que é geada ou nev'e nom al.

"With his books this clever dean
can even cure St. Anthony's fire:
should a woman catch this disease,
with his fucking he can charm her
until the fire burns so low
that all she feels is frost or snow."

59.

ALFONSO X, KING OF CASTILE AND LEÓN

cantiga de amigo

Ai eu coitada, como vivo em gram cuidado
por meu amigo que hei alongado.
Muito me tarda
o meu amigo na Guarda.

Ai eu coitada, como vivo em gram desejo
por meu amigo que tarda e nom vejo.
Muito me tarda
o meu amigo na Guarda.

59.

ALFONSO X, KING OF CASTILE AND LEÓN

Song for a Beloved in Guarda

Oh! what agony, always the ache
for my beloved, who went away.
How much longer
will he stay in Guarda?

Oh! what torment always to yearn
for my beloved to return.
How much longer
will he stay in Guarda?

60.

MARTIM CODAX

cantiga de amigo

Ondas do mar de Vigo,
se vistes meu amigo?
    E ai Deus, se verrá cedo?

Ondas do mar levado,
se vistes meu amado?
    E ai Deus, se verrá cedo?

Se vistes meu amigo,
o por que eu sospiro?
    E ai Deus, se verrá cedo?

Se vistes meu amado,
o por que hei gram coidado?
    E ai Deus, se verrá cedo?

60.

MARTIM CODAX

Seven Songs for a Beloved in Vigo

ONE

Sea waves at Vigo,
have you seen my beloved?
    Oh God! Is he coming?

Sea waves that swell,
have you seen my friend?
    Oh God! Is he coming?

Have you seen my beloved
who makes my heart troubled?
    Oh God! Is he coming?

Have you seen my friend
who makes my heart fret?
    Oh God! Is he coming?

61.

MARTIM CODAX

cantiga de amigo

Mandad'hei comigo
ca vem meu amigo,
   e irei, madr', a Vigo.

Comig'hei mandado
ca vem meu amado,
   e irei, madr', a Vigo.

Ca vem meu amigo
e vem san'e vivo,
   e irei, madr', a Vigo.

Ca vem meu amado
e vem viv'e sano,
   e irei, madr', a Vigo.

Ca vem san'e vivo
e d'el-rei amigo,
   e irei, madr', a Vigo.

Ca vem vivo e sano
e d'el-rei privado,
   e irei, madr', a Vigo.

61.

MARTIM CODAX

TWO

Word came today:
my friend's on his way,
   and, Mother, I'm going to Vigo.

Today came the tidings:
my friend is arriving,
   and, Mother, I'm going to Vigo.

My friend's on his way,
he's alive and well,
   and, Mother, I'm going to Vigo.

My friend is arriving,
he's well and alive,
   and, Mother, I'm going to Vigo.

He's alive and well,
the king is his friend,
   and, Mother, I'm going to Vigo.

He's well and alive,
he's the king's close ally,
   and, Mother, I'm going to Vigo.

62.

MARTIM CODAX

cantiga de amigo

Mia irmana fremosa, treides comigo
a la igreja de Vigo u é o mar salido
e miraremos las ondas.

Mia irmana fremosa, treides de grado
a la igreja de Vigo u é o mar levado
e miraremos las ondas.

A la igreja de Vigo u é o mar levado
e verrá i, mia madre, o meu amado
e miraremos las ondas.

A la igreja de Vigo u é o mar salido
e verrá i, mia madre, o meu amigo
e miraremos las ondas.

62.

MARTIM CODAX

THREE

Come along, Sister, come with me now
to the church in Vigo, where the waters pound,
   and we'll look at the waves.

Come with me, Sister, to spend some time
at the church in Vigo, where the sea is high,
   and we'll look at the waves.

To the church in Vigo, where the sea is high,
my friend, dear Mother, will soon come by,
   and we'll look at the waves.

To the church in Vigo, where the waters pound,
my friend, dear Mother, will soon come around,
   and we'll look at the waves.

63.

MARTIM CODAX

cantiga de amigo

Ai Deus, se sab'ora meu amigo
com'eu senheira estou em Vigo!
E vou namorada . . .

Ai Deus, se sab'ora meu amado
com'eu em Vigo senheira manho!
E vou namorada . . .

Com'eu senheira estou em Vigo
e nulhas gardas nom hei comigo!
E vou namorada . . .

Com'eu senheira em Vigo manho
e nulhas gardas migo nom trago!
E vou namorada . . .

E nulhas gardas nom hei comigo,
ergas meus olhos que choram migo!
E vou namorada . . .

E nulhas gardas migo nom trago,
ergas meus olhos que choram ambos!
E vou namorada . . .

63.

MARTIM CODAX

FOUR

Oh God, does my beloved know
I'm here in Vigo all alone
    and so in love?

Oh God, does he know I've arrived,
alone in Vigo to spend the night
    and so in love?

I'm here in Vigo all alone,
unguarded by a chaperone
    and so in love . . .

Alone in Vigo to spend the night
under no one's watchful sight
    and so in love . . .

Unguarded by a chaperone,
my eyes are crying on their own,
    and so in love . . .

Under no one's watchful sight,
alone my eyes will cry all night,
    and so in love . . .

64.

MARTIM CODAX

cantiga de amigo

Quantas sabedes amar amigo,
treides comig'a lo mar de Vigo
   e banhar-nos-emos nas ondas.

Quantas sabedes amar amado,
treides comig' a lo mar levado
   e banhar-nos-emos nas ondas.

Treides comig' a lo mar de Vigo
e veeremo' lo meu amigo
   e banhar-nos-emos nas ondas.

Treides comig' a lo mar levado
e veeremo' lo meu amado
   e banhar-nos-emos nas ondas.

64.

MARTIM CODAX

FIVE

You girls who know what it means to love,
come with me to the sea at Vigo,
    and we'll bathe in the waves.

You girls who know what loving means,
come with me to the swollen sea,
    and we'll bathe in the waves.

Come with me to the sea at Vigo
and there we'll see the one I love,
    and we'll bathe in the waves.

Come with me to the swollen sea
and there we'll see the one I mean,
    and we'll bathe in the waves.

65.

MARTIM CODAX

cantiga de amigo

Eno sagrado em Vigo
bailava corpo velido.
Amor hei!

Em Vigo, no sagrado,
bailava corpo delgado.
Amor hei!

Bailava corpo velido
que nunc'houver'amigo.
Amor hei!

Bailava corpo delgado
que nunc'houver'amado.
Amor hei!

Que nunc'houver'amigo
ergas no sagrad'em Vigo.
Amor hei!

Que nunc'houver'amado
ergas em Vigo no sagrado.
Amor hei!

65.

MARTIM CODAX

SIX

In Vigo next to the belfry
I danced, a lovely body.
I've fallen in love!

Next to the belfry in Vigo
I danced, a slender figure.
I've fallen in love!

I danced, a slender figure
who never had a beloved.
I've fallen in love!

I danced, a lovely body
who never had a boyfriend.
I've fallen in love!

Who never had a boyfriend
till Vigo, next to the belfry.
I've fallen in love!

Who never had a beloved
till next to the belfry in Vigo.
I've fallen in love!

66.

MARTIM CODAX

cantiga de amigo

Ai ondas que eu vim veer,
se me saberedes dizer
    por que tarda meu amigo sem mim?

Ai ondas que eu vim mirar,
se me saberedes contar
    por que tarda meu amigo sem mim?

66.

MARTIM CODAX

SEVEN

Oh waves I've come to see,
do you know the reason
   my beloved tarries without me?

Oh waves I've come to watch,
can you tell me why
   my beloved tarries without me?

67.

MEENDINHO

cantiga de amigo

Sedia-m'eu na ermida de Sam Simion
e cercarom-mi as ondas, que grandes som.
Eu atendendo meu amig', eu atendendo.

Estando na ermida ant'o altar
e cercarom-mi as ondas grandes do mar.
Eu atendendo meu amig', eu atendendo.

E cercarom-mi as ondas, que grandes som.
Nom hei eu i barqueiro nem remador.
Eu atendendo meu amig', eu atendendo.

E cercarom-mi as ondas do alto mar;
nom hei eu i barqueiro nem sei remar.
Eu atendendo meu amig', eu atendendo.

Nom hei eu i barqueiro nem remador
e morrerei fremosa no mar maior.
Eu atendendo meu amig', eu atendendo.

Nom hei eu i barqueiro nem sei remar
e morrerei fremosa no alto mar.
Eu atendendo meu amig', eu atendendo.

67.

Song of a Girl Still Waiting

Sitting in the chapel of San Simón,
soon I was surrounded by the rising ocean,
  waiting for my lover, still waiting.

Before the altar of the chapel, waiting,
soon I was surrounded by the ocean's waves,
  waiting for my lover, still waiting.

Soon I was surrounded by the rising ocean,
without a boatman, unused to rowing,
  waiting for my lover, still waiting.

Soon I was surrounded by the ocean's waves,
without a boatman to row me away,
  waiting for my lover, still waiting.

Without a boatman, unused to rowing,
I'll die, a fair girl, in the heaving ocean,
  waiting for my lover, still waiting.

Without a boatman to row me away,
I'll die, a fair girl, in the ocean's waves,
  waiting for my lover, still waiting.

68.

PERO GOMES BARROSO

cantiga moral

Do que sabia nulha rem nom sei,
polo mundo, que vej'assi andar;
e quand'i cuido, hei log'a cuidar,
per boa fé, o que nunca cuidei:
　　ca vej'agora o que nunca vi
　　e ouço cousas que nunca oí.

Aquesto mundo, par Deus, nom é tal
qual eu vi outro, nom há gram sazom,
e por aquesto, no meu coraçom,
aquel desej'e este quero mal:
　　ca vej'agora o que nunca vi
　　e ouço cousas que nunca oí.

E nom receo mia morte por en
e, Deus lo sabe, queria morrer,
ca nom vejo de que haja prazer
nem sei amigo de que diga bem:
　　ca vej'agora o que nunca vi
　　e ouço cousas que nunca oí.

E se me a mim Deus quisess'atender,
per boa fé, ũa pouca razom,
eu post'havia no meu coraçom
de nunca jamais nẽum bem fazer:
　　ca vej'agora o que nunca vi
　　e ouço cousas que nunca oí.

E nom daria rem por viver i
en'este mundo mais do que vivi.

68.

PERO GOMES BARROSO

Song about a Worsening World

Things I knew I know no longer
in this world that's changed so much,
and thinking about it I find I must
think in ways I've never thought,
    as I'm seeing things I've never seen
    and hearing things I've never heard.

This world, by God, is not the place
it was when I was still a youth,
and in my heart, to tell the truth,
I love that old world, not today's,
    as I'm seeing things I've never seen
    and hearing things I've never heard.

I have no reason to fear death
and, God knows, I'd like to die,
as there's no pleasure in this life
and no one who's my faithful friend.
    I'm seeing things I've never seen
    and hearing things I've never heard.

I hope and pray God will accept
the way I think for my own part,
as I've decided in my heart
never to do good works again,
    as I'm seeing things I've never seen
    and hearing things I've never heard.

And I wouldn't give two cents to live
more years here than those I've lived.

69.

ROI PAIS DE RIBELA

cantiga de escárnio

Vem um ric'home das truitas
que compra duas por muitas,
e coz'end'a ũa.

Por quanto xi quer ebenas,
compra en duas pequenas,
e coz'end'a ũa.

Vendem cem truitas vivas,
e compra en duas cativas,
e coz'end'a ũa.

E u as vendem bolindo,
vai-s'en com duas riindo
e coz'end'a ũa.

69.

ROI PAIS DE RIBELA

Song about a Rich Man's Trout

A rich man buying trout
buys two (and that's a lot!)
   and cooks one of them.

Although he likes big fish,
he buys two of the littlest
   and cooks one of them.

They sell trout freshly caught,
but he buys two about to rot
   and cooks one of them.

Where a hundred can be had
he buys two and is glad
   and cooks one of them.

70.

cantiga de escárnio

Preguntad'um ric'home
mui rico, que mal come:
　　por que o faz?

El de fam'e de sede
mata home, ben'o sabede.
　　Por que o faz?

Mal com'e faz nemiga.
Dizede-lhi que diga
　　porque o faz.

70.

Song about a Rich Nobleman

Ask a rich nobleman
who eats what's unwholesome:
    what for?

His thirst and his hunger
lead him to kill others.
    What for?

He eats and acts badly,
so go and ask him:
    what for?

71.

ROI PAIS DE RIBELA

cantiga de escárnio

A donzela de Biscaia
ainda mi a preito saia
de noit'ou lũar!

Pois m'agora assi desdenha,
ainda mi a preito venha
de noit'ou lũar!

Pois dela sõo maltreito,
ainda mi venha a preito
de noit'ou lũar!

71.

ROI PAIS DE RIBELA

Song about a Disdainful Damsel

May the damsel of Biscay
still do me a favor today
    under the light of the moon!

Although she now disdains me,
I hope she's ready and waiting
    under the light of the moon!

Although she treats me badly,
I'm hoping she'll still have me
    under the light of the moon!

72.

JOAM VASQUES DE TALAVEIRA

cantiga de escárnio

O que veer quiser, ai cavaleiro,
Maria Pérez, leve algum dinheiro,
senom nom poderá i adubar prol.

Quen'a veer quiser ao serão,
Maria Pérez, lev'alg'em sa mão,
senom nom poderá i adubar prol.

Tod'home que a ir queira veer suso,
Maria Pérez, lev'algo de juso,
senom nom poderá i adubar prol.

72.

Song about How to Enjoy a Dancer

If you're a gentlemen planning to see
Maria Perez, take some money,
or you're not going to get very far.

If you're going to the evening dance
of Maria Perez, have something in hand,
or you're not going to get very far.

If, after the show, you want to converse
with Maria Perez, take a full purse,
or you're not going to get very far.

73.

LOURENÇO

cantiga de amigo

Três moças cantavam d'amor,
mui fremosinhas pastores,
mui coitadas dos amores.
E diss'end'ũa, mia senhor:
—Dized'amigas comigo
o cantar do meu amigo.

Todas três cantavam mui bem,
come moças namoradas
e dos amores coitadas.
E diss'a por que perço o sem
—Dized'amigas comigo
o cantar do meu amigo.

Que gram sabor eu havia
de as oir cantar entom!
E prougue-mi de coraçom
quanto mia senhor dizia:
—Dized'amigas comigo
o cantar do meu amigo.

E se as eu mais oísse,
a que gram sabor estava!
E quam muito me pagava
de como mia senhor disse:
—Dized'amigas comigo
o cantar do meu amigo.

73.

LOURENÇO

Song about Three Girls Singing

Three maidens were singing of love,
all of them beautiful girls,
all very in love and hurting.
And the one who's my lady implored:
    "Sing with me, friends,
    my boyfriend's song!"

In singing they all excelled,
like girls who have beloveds
and hurt since they're so in love.
And the one I'm mad for exclaimed:
    "Sing with me, friends,
    my boyfriend's song!"

Imagine how it pleased me
to hear them sing it so well!
And it caused my heart to swell
when I heard my lady plead:
    "Sing with me, friends,
    my boyfriend's song!"

I could have kept on listening
with nothing but enjoyment,
and what I most enjoyed
was to hear my lady insisting:
    "Sing with me, friends,
    my boyfriend's song!"

74.

LOURENÇO AND JOAM VASQUES
DE TALAVEIRA

tenção

—Joam Vaásquez, moiro por saber
de vós por que leixastes o trobar
ou se foi el vos primeiro leixar,
ca vedes o que ouço a todos dizer:
ca o trobar acordou-s'em atal:
que 'stava vosco em pecado mortal
e leixa-vos, por se nom perder.

—Lourenço, tu veens por aprender
de mim, e eu nom cho quero negar:
eu trobo bem quando quero trobar,
pero nom o quero sempre fazer.
Mais di-me ti, que trobas desigual,
se te deitam por en de Portugal,
ou se matast'hom', ou roubast'haver.

—Joam Vaásquez, nunca roubei rem,
nem matei homem, nem ar mereci
porque mi deitassem, mais vim aqui
por gaar algo, e pois sei iguar-mi bem
como o trobar vosso. Mais estou
que se perdia convosc'e quitou-
-se de vós, e nom trobades por en.

74.

LOURENÇO AND JOAM VASQUES
DE TALAVEIRA

Song of the Troubadour's Art on Finding Itself in Sin

—Joam Vasques, I'm dying to know
why you've let go of the troubadours' art,
or is it, as people here have remarked,
that the art of troubadours let you go?
They say our art, with great chagrin,
saw you had led it into mortal sin
and shunned you to avoid eternal woe.

—*Lourenço, you misunderstand:*
I still make excellent troubadour songs
but only when the urge is strong.
And tell me now, if you can,
you, a poet who can't count syllables:
is that why they ran you out of Portugal,
or because you robbed or killed a man?

—Joam Vasques, I've done no wrong
to any man that I would ever deserve
to be sent into exile. I'm here to earn
some money, as I'm quite good at counting
syllables in my songs. But it seems
the troubadours' art, fleeing from sin,
has left you. And so you write no songs.

75.

JOAM BAVECA

cantiga de amor

Os que nom amam nem sabem d'amor
fazem perder aos que amor ham.
Vedes porquê: quand'ant'as donas vam,
juram que morrem por elas d'amor,
e elas sabem pois que nom é 'ssi;
    e por esto perç'eu e os que bem
    lealmente amam, segundo meu sem.

Ca se elas soubessem os que ham
bem verdadeiramente grand'amor,
d'alguém se doeria sa senhor;
mais, por aqueles que o jurad'ham,
cuidam-s'elas que todos taes som;
    e por esto perç'eu e os que bem
    lealmente amam, segundo meu sem.

E aqueles que já medo nom ham
que lhis faça coita sofrer amor,
vêm ant'elas e juram melhor
ou tam bem come os que amor ham,
e elas nom sabem quaes creer;
    e por esto perç'eu e os que bem
    lealmente amam, segundo meu sem.

. . .

75.

JOAM BAVECA

Song against Those Who Falsely Swear Love

Those whose love is merely feigned
do wrong to us who truly love.
Gallantly going up to the ladies,
they swear they're dying of love for them,
and the ladies know it isn't so,
        and that is why, without a doubt,
        we who truly love lose out.

If they knew the pure intention
of those of us whose love is true,
these ladies would I'm sure be moved,
but those who falsely swear affection
make them think we're all that way,
        and that is why, without a doubt,
        we who truly love lose out.

Those who do not need to fear
that love might ever make them suffer
can swear devotion just as much
or more than those who truly feel,
and the ladies don't know whom to believe,
        and that is why, without a doubt,
        we who truly love lose out.

. . .

E os bem desamparados d'amor
juram que morrem com amor que ham,
seend'ant'elas, e mentem de pram;
mais, quand'ar vêm os que ham amor,
já elas cuidam que vêm mentir;
    e por esto perç'eu e os que bem
    lealmente amam, segundo meu sem.

Those whose love is insincere
swear they love to the point of dying
before the ladies, boldly lying,
and as for those who love sincerely,
the ladies think we're lying too,
    and that is why, without a doubt,
    we who truly love lose out.

76.

JOAM BAVECA

cantiga de amigo

—Filha, de grado queria saber
de voss'amig'e de vós ũa rem:
como vos vai ou como vos avém.
  —Eu vo-lo quero, mia madre, dizer:
    quero-lh'eu bem e que-lo el a mi
    e bem vos digo que nom há mais i.

—Filha, nom sei se há i mais, se nom,
mais vejo-vos sempre com el falar
e vejo-vos chorar e el chorar.
  —Nom vos terrei, madre, i outra razom:
    quero-lh'eu bem e que-lo el a mi
    e bem vos digo que nom há mais i.

—Se mi o negardes, filha, pesar-mi-á,
ca, se mais há i feit', a como quer,
outro conselh'havemos i mester.
  —Já vos eu dixi, madre, quant'i há:
    quero-lh'eu bem e que-lo el a mi
    e bem vos digo que nom há mais i.

76.

JOAM BAVECA

Song about a Suspicious Mother

—Daughter, please, I'd like to know
something about you and your friend:
how does it go, and where will it end?
—*I'll tell you, Mother, how it goes:*
he loves me, and I love him,
and I swear that's all there is.

—I wonder, Daughter, if there's more,
for every time your friend comes by
I see you weep and see him cry.
—*Mother, it's like I said before:*
he loves me, and I love him,
and I swear that's all there is.

—Beloved Daughter, I'll be upset
if there's more than what you've told me,
since then we'd need to act more boldly.
—*Mother, it's like I already said:*
he loves me, and I love him,
and I swear that's all there is.

77.

PERO MEOGO

cantiga de amigo

Levou-s'aa alva, levou-s'a velida,
vai lavar cabelos na fontana fria;
leda dos amores, dos amores leda.

Levou-s'aa alva, levou-s'a louçana,
vai lavar cabelos na fria fontana;
leda dos amores, dos amores leda.

Vai lavar cabelos na fontana fria,
passou seu amigo, que lhi bem queria;
leda dos amores, dos amores leda.

Vai lavar cabelos na fria fontana,
passa seu amigo, que a muit'amava;
leda dos amores, dos amores leda.

Passa seu amigo, que lhi bem queria,
o cervo do monte a áugua volvia;
leda dos amores, dos amores leda.

Passa seu amigo que a muit'amava,
o cervo do monte volvia a áugua;
leda dos amores, dos amores leda.

77.

Song about a Girl at a Spring

She awoke at dawn, she woke up fair;
she goes to the spring to wash her hair.
  Happily in love, in love she's happy.

She awoke at dawn, she woke up pretty;
she goes to the spring—her hair needs washing.
  Happily in love, in love she's happy.

She goes to the spring to wash her hair;
the boy who loves her met her there.
  Happily in love, in love she's happy.

She goes to the spring—her hair needs washing;
there she meets the boy who loves her.
  Happily in love, in love she's happy.

The boy who loves her meets here there;
the mountain stag made the water stir.
  Happily in love, in love she's happy.

There she meets the boy who loves her;
the mountain stag stirred up the water.
  Happily in love, in love she's happy.

78.

PERO MEOGO

cantiga de amigo

—Digades, filha, mia filha velida,
por que tardastes na fontana fria?
 —Os amores hei.

—Digades, filha, mia filha louçana,
por que tardastes na fria fontana?
 —Os amores hei.

—Tardei, mia madre, na fontana fria,
cervos do monte a áugua volviam.
 Os amores hei.

Tardei, mia madre, na fria fontana,
cervos do monte volviam a áugua.
 Os amores hei.

—Mentir, mia filha, mentir por amigo,
nunca vi cervo que volvesse o rio.
 —Os amores hei.

—Mentir, mia filha, mentir por amado,
nunca vi cervo que volvess'o alto;
 —Os amores hei.

78.

PERO MEOGO

Song about a Girl Back from the Spring

Tell me, Daughter, my beautiful daughter,
why you tarried at the cold spring.
  I'm in love.

Tell me, Daughter, my daughter so fair,
why at that cold spring you tarried.
  I'm in love.

I tarried, Mother, at the cold spring,
as mountain stags set the waters astir.
  I'm in love.

At that cold spring, Mother, I tarried,
as mountain stags stirred up the waters.
  I'm in love.

You're lying, Daughter, lying for your friend:
I've never seen stags stir up the stream.
  I'm in love.

You're lying, Daughter, lying for your lover:
I've never seen stags stir up the river.
  I'm in love.

79.

PERO MEOGO

cantiga de amigo

—Tal vai o meu amigo, com amor que lh'eu dei,
come cervo ferido de monteiro del-rei.

Tal vai o meu amigo, madre, com meu amor,
come cervo ferido de monteiro maior.

E se el vai ferido, irá morrer al mar;
'si fará meu amigo, se eu del nom pensar.

—E guardade-vos, filha, ca já m'eu atal vi
que se fezo coitado por gaanhar de mim.

E guardade-vos, filha, ca já m'eu vi atal
que se fezo coitado por de mim guaanhar.

79.

PERO MEOGO

Song about an Endangered Friend

—With the love I gave him there goes my friend,
like a stag wounded by a huntsman of the king.

There goes my friend with my love, dear Mother,
like a stag wounded by the king's chief hunter.

And if he goes wounded, then at sea he'll die;
I must cherish my friend, to preserve him alive.

—*Take care, dear Daughter: I have seen such a man
who made me feel pity to win an advantage.*

*Take care, dear Daughter: such a man I have seen
who made me feel pity to take advantage of me.*

80.

PEDRO AMGIO DE SEVILHA

cantiga de amigo

Moir', amiga, desejando
meu amig', e vós no vosso
mi falades, e nom posso
estar sempr'en'esto falando.
    Mais queredes falar migo?
    Falemos no meu amigo.

Queredes que todavia
eno voss'amigo fale
vosc'e, se nom, que me cale;
e nom poss'eu cada dia.
    Mais queredes falar migo?
    Falemos no meu amigo.

Amiga, sempre queredes
que fale vosc'e falades
no voss'amig', e cuidades
que poss'eu. Non'o cuidedes.
    Mais queredes falar migo?
    Falemos no meu amigo.

Nom havedes d'al cuidado,
sol que eu vosco bem diga
do voss'amig', e, amiga,
nom poss'eu, nem é guisado.
    Mais queredes falar migo?
    Falemos no meu amigo.

80.

PEDRO AMIGO DE SEVILHA

Song about Two Girls Talking

Here I am dying of desire
for my friend while you, Sister,
just talk of yours, and I'm tired
of so much talk about him.
    If you want to converse,
    let my friend come first.

You expect me to keep on talking
about nothing but your friend
—either that, or hold my tongue.
And it's like this for days on end.
    If you want to converse,
    let my friend come first.

You're always talking, Sister,
and counting on me to talk too
about your friend, and you think
I don't mind at all, but I do.
    If you want to converse,
    let my friend come first.

Whether, Sister, I speak well
of your friend is your only care,
as far as I can tell,
but I'm fed up—it's not fair!
    If you want to converse,
    let my friend come first.

81.

ROI FERNANDES DE SANTIAGO

cantiga de amor

Quand'eu vejo las ondas
e las muit'altas ribas,
logo mi vêm ondas
al cor, pola velida:
    maldito seja'l mare
    que mi faz tanto male!

Nunca vejo las ondas
nen'as altas debrocas
que mi nom venham ondas
al cor, pola fremosa:
    maldito seja'l mare
    que mi faz tanto male!

Se eu vejo las ondas
e vejo las costeiras,
logo mi vêm ondas
al cor, pola bem feita:
    maldito seja'l mare
    que mi faz tanto male!

81.

ROI FERNANDES DE SANTIAGO

Song against the Sea

Whenever I look at the waves
that break against the bluffs,
I feel a pounding of waves
in my heart for the one I love.
    Damn the sea
    that makes me grieve!

I never look at the waves
that pummel the rocky shores
without being pounded by waves
in my heart for the one I adore.
    Damn the sea
    that makes me grieve!

Each time I look at the waves
that crash against the cliffs,
I feel a pounding of waves
in my heart for the one I miss.
    Damn the sea
    that makes me grieve!

82.

ROI FERNANDES DE SANTIAGO

cantiga de amor

Ora começa o meu mal
de que já nom temia rem,
e cuidava que m'ia bem.
E todo se tornou em mal,
    ca o dem'agora d'amor
    me fez filhar outra senhor.

E já dormia tod'o meu
sono e já nom era fol
e podia fazer mia prol.
Mais lo poder já nom é meu,
    ca o dem'agora d'amor
    me fez filhar outra senhor.

Que ledo me fezera já,
quando s'Amor de mim quitou
um pouco, que mi a mim leixou.
Mais doutra guisa me vai já,
    ca o dem'agora d'amor
    me fez filhar outra senhor.

E nom se dev'hom'alegrar
muito de rem que poss'haver,
ca eu, que o quige fazer,
nom hei já de que m'alegrar,
    ca o dem'agora d'amor
    me fez filhar outra senhor!

. . .

82.

ROI FERNANDES DE SANTIAGO

Song of a Man in Trouble

Now begin my troubles,
which seemed to be behind me.
Life was treating me kindly,
but then I ran into trouble,
   the demon of Love having led me
   to serve yet another lady.

I'd learned once more to rule
my life, to tame my mind
and to sleep the entire night,
but then I was overruled,
   the demon of Love having led me
   to serve yet another lady.

All my happiness returned
the very same day that Love
began to leave me alone,
but now the tables are turned,
   the demon of Love having led me
   to serve yet another lady.

A man should never say
he's happy with what he has.
I thought I could be happy
but didn't have the final say,
   the demon of Love having led me
   to serve yet another lady.

. . .

Ao dem'acomend'eu Amor;
e bẽeiga Deus a senhor
de que nom será sabedor
nulh'hom', enquant'eu vivo for.

Love can go to the devil,
but may God bless my lady,
whose name I'll never reveal
for as long as I am living.

83.

JOAM LOBEIRA

cantiga de amor

Senhor genta,
mi tormenta
voss'amor em guisa tal,
que tormenta
que eu senta
outra nom m'é bem nem mal,
mais la vossa m'é mortal.
    Leonoreta,
    fin roseta,
    bela sobre toda fror,
    fin roseta,
    nom me meta
    em tal coita voss'amor!

Das que vejo
nom desejo
outra senhor se vós nom,
e desejo
tam sobejo
mataria um leom,
senhor do meu coraçom!
    Leonoreta,
    fin roseta,
    bela sobre toda fror,
    fin roseta,
    nom me meta
    em tal coita voss'amor!

. . .

83.

JOAM LOBEIRA

Song for Leonorette

Lovely lady,
you torment me
with your love in such a way
my mind, tormented,
can't remember
other loves from former days:
your love's fatal, I'm afraid.
    Leonorette,
    fine rosette,
    lovelier than any flower;
    fine rosette,
    do not let
    me fall too far into your power!

I admire
but don't desire
any lady but you alone,
and this desire
is so on fire
it could bring a lion down,
lady whom my heart enthrones!
    Leonorette,
    fine rosette,
    lovelier than any flower;
    fine rosette,
    do not let
    me fall too far into your power!

. . .

Mia ventura
em loucura
me meteu de vos amar;
é loucura
que me dura,
que me nom posso en quitar,
ai fremosura sem par!
    Leonoreta,
    fin roseta,
    bela sobre toda fror,
    fin roseta,
    nom me meta
    em tal coita voss'amor!

It was chance that
acting madly
made me fall in love with you,
and the madness
keeps on lasting:
there is nothing I can do
before such beauty, pure and true!
  Leonorette,
  fine rosette,
  lovelier than any flower;
  fine rosette,
  do not let
  me fall too far into your power!

84.

cantiga de amigo

Pois nossas madres vam a Sam Simom
de Val de Prados candeas queimar,
nós, as meninhas, punhemos d'andar
com nossas madres, e elas entom
queimem candeas por nós e por si,
e nós, meninhas, bailaremos i.

Nossos amigos todos lá irám
por nos veer e andaremos nós
bailand'ant'eles fremosas em cós,
e nossas madres, pois que alá vam,
queimem candeas por nós e por si.
e nós, meninhas, bailaremos i.

Nossos amigos irám por cousir
como bailamos e podem veer
bailar i moças de bom parecer,
e nossas madres, pois lá querem ir,
queimem candeas por nós e por si,
e nós, meninhas, bailaremos i.

84.

PERO VIVIÃES

Song in Favor of a Pilgrimage

Since our mothers are going to St. Simon's
in Val de Prados to light votive candles,
let's go, girls, and visit the shrine
along with our mothers, who inside the chapel
    can light candles for our souls and theirs
    while we girls dance in the open air.

Since our boyfriends will all be there
just to be able to see us, let's go
and dance, shedding our capes to look fair.
Our mothers will also be there and so
    can light candles for our souls and theirs
    while we girls dance in the open air.

Our boyfriends, who'll be there to see
how well we dance, can enjoy the view
of our dancing figures, our girlish beauty.
As for our mothers, who'll be there too,
    they can light candles for our souls and theirs
    while we girls dance in the open air.

85.

AIRAS NUNES

cantiga de amigo

Bailemos nós já todas três, ai amigas,
sô aquestas avelaneiras frolidas,
e quem for velida, como nós, velidas,
   se amigo amar,
sô aquestas avelaneiras frolidas
   verrá bailar.

Bailemos nós já todas três, ai irmanas,
sô aqueste ramo destas avelanas,
e quem for louçana, como nós, louçanas,
   se amigo amar,
sô aqueste ramo destas avelanas
   verrá bailar.

Por Deus, ai amigas, mentr'al nom fazemos
sô aqueste ramo frolido bailemos,
e quem bem parecer, como nós parecemos,
   se amigo amar,
sô aqueste ramo, sol que nós bailemos,
   verrá bailar.

85.

AIRAS NUNES

Song of the Flowering Hazel Trees

Come on, you two, and dance with me,
under these flowering hazel trees,
and other girls who, like us, are pretty
    and truly in love
    will dance with us
under these flowering hazel trees.

Why don't we dance as a threesome, friends,
under these hazel trees in flower?
And other girls who, like us, are fair
    and truly in love
    will dance with us
under these hazel trees in flower.

Girls, while we've nothing better to do,
let's dance under these trees in bloom,
and other girls who, like us, are beautiful
    and truly in love
    will dance with us
under these hazel trees in bloom.

86.

AIRAS NUNES

cantiga moral

Porque no mundo mengou a verdade,
punhei um dia de a ir buscar,
e, u por ela fui a preguntar,
disserom todos: —Alhur la buscade,
ca de tal guisa se foi a perder
que nom podemos en novas haver,
nem já nom anda na irmaindade.

Nos moesteiros dos frades negrados
a demandei, e disserom-m'assi:
—Nom busquedes vós a verdad'aqui,
ca muitos anos havemos passados
que nom morou nosco, per bõa fé,
nem sabemos u ela agora x'é,
e d'al havemos maiores coidados.

E em Cistel, u verdade soía
sempre morar, disserom-me que nom
morava i havia gram sazom,
nem frade d'i já a nom conhocia,
nem o abade outrossi, no estar,
sol nom queria que foss'i pousar,
e anda já fora da abadia.

. . .

244

86.

AIRAS NUNES

Song in Search of Truth

Since truth was missing from the world
I decided to go and look for her,
calling at various religious orders.
They all answered, "Go look elsewhere.
Long ago she left our midst
and doesn't even come for visits
nor any longer send us word."

In abbeys where black habits are used
I asked for her, and the monks replied:
"Asking us is a waste of time,
as many years have passed since truth
dwelled among us, nor do we know
or worry about where she is now.
We've got better things to do."

In Cîteaux, where white is preferred,
truth had long resided but left
—so I was told. The monks I met
had never been acquainted with her,
and the abbot said, "I wouldn't allow
her back, not even in the guest house.
She's gone for good and can't return."

. . .

Em Santiago, seend'albergado
em mia pousada, chegarom romeus.
Preguntei-os e disserom: —Par Deus,
muito levade'lo caminh'errado!
Ca, se verdade quiserdes achar,
outro caminho convém a buscar,
ca nom sabem aqui dela mandado.

I stayed at a hospice in Santiago,
where I met some pilgrims and explained
my quest. "For God's sake," they said,
"you've come a long way on the wrong road!
If truth is really your aspiration,
you'll have to search in other places.
She left this town a long time ago."

87.

AIRAS NUNES

pastorela

Oí hoj'eu ũa pastor cantar
u cavalgava per ũa ribeira,
e a pastor estava senlheira
e ascondi-me pola ascuitar,
e dizia mui bem este cantar:
   "Sô lo ramo verd'e frolido
   vodas fazem a meu amigo,
   e choram olhos d'amor."

E a pastor parecia mui bem,
e chorava e estava cantando,
e eu mui passo fui-mi achegando
pola oír e sol nom falei rem,
e dizia este cantar mui bem:
   "Ai estorninho do avelanedo,
   cantades vós e moir'eu e pen'
   e d'amores hei mal."

E eu oí-a sospirar entom,
e queixava-se estando com amores,
e fazi'ũa guirlanda de flores,
des i chorava mui de coraçom
e dizia este cantar entom:
   "Que coita hei tam grande de sofrer:
   amar amig'e non'ousar veer!
   E pousarei sô lo avelanal."

. . .

248

87.

AIRAS NUNES

Pastoral Song

Today I heard a shepherdess singing
as I rode alongside a river;
she was alone, no one was with her,
and I kept hidden, to listen.
This is the song she sang:
   "Under the flowering branch
   my beloved is getting married,
   and my eyes are crying with love!"

She was a beautiful shepherdess
and sang, but she was crying,
and little by little I drew close by
to listen, not making a whisper,
and the song she sang was this:
   "Oh starling of the hazelnut grove,
   you sing while I die of sorrow,
   hurting because I'm in love!"

Then I heard the shepherdess sighing,
complaining of love and its sorrows
while she wove a wreath of flowers.
Soon she burst out crying,
and this is what I heard her singing:
   "What torment this is: to dare not see
   my dearly beloved!
   I'll rest beneath the hazelnut trees."

. . .

Pois que a guirlanda fez a pastor,
foi-se cantando, indo s'en manselinho,
e tornei-m'eu logo a meu caminho,
ca de a nojar nom houve sabor,
e dizia este cantar bem a pastor:
    "Pela ribeira do rio
    cantando ia la virgo
    d'amor:
        'Quem amores há
        como dormirá,
        ai bela frol?' "

After weaving her wreath, forever
singing she went on her way,
and I went back to my own way,
not wishing to disturb her,
and this is the song I heard:
    "Along the bank of the river
    went a young girl singing
    of love:
        'Oh sweet flower,
        how can anyone
        sleep when in love?' "

88.

AIRAS NUNES

cantiga de amor

Que muito m'eu pago deste verão,
por estes ramos e por estas flores
e polas aves que cantam d'amores,
por que ando i led'e sem cuidado,
e assi faz tod'homem namorado:
sempre i anda led'e mui loução.

Cand'eu passo per algũas ribeiras,
sô bõas árvores, per bõos prados,
se cantam i pássaros namorados,
log'eu com amores i vou cantando,
e log'ali d'amores vou trobando
e faço cantares em mil maneiras.

Hei eu gram viço e grand'alegria
quando mi as aves cantam no estio.

88.

AIRAS NUNES

Song of Love in the Summer

How very much I love this summer,
its leafy boughs, its vivid flowers
and all the birds that sing of love,
because I feel at peace and happy
and even handsome—that's what happens
whenever we're in love with someone.

When I walk along certain streams,
beneath fair trees or in fair meadows,
if mating birds sing sweet melodies
then with love and all my heart
and all I know of troubadour art
I compose myriad musical themes.

I feel joyous, free of troubles,
when I hear birds sing in summer.

89.

PAIO GOMES CHARINHO

cantiga de amor

Ũa dona que eu quero gram bem,
por mal de mi, par Deus, que nom por al,
pero que sempre mi fez e faz mal
e fará, direi-vo-lo que m'avém:
  mar, nem terra, nem prazer, nem pesar,
  nem bem, nem mal, nom mi a podem quitar

do coraçom. E que será de mim?
Morto sõo, se cedo nom morrer.
Ela já nunca bem mi há de fazer,
mais sempre mal, e pero est assi:
  mar, nem terra, nem prazer, nem pesar,
  nem bem, nem mal, nom mi a podem quitar

do coraçom. Ora mi vai peior,
ca mi vem dela, por vos nom mentir,
mal se a vej', e mal se a nom vir,
que de coitas mais cuido a maior:
  mar, nem terra, nem prazer, nem pesar,
  nem bem, nem mal, nom mi a podem quitar.

89.

PAIO GOMES CHARINHO

Song about an Occupied Heart

There's a woman I love hopelessly
(God knows why but for my own disgrace),
who always was and is and will be
a source of pain I can't erase,
  since neither sea nor land nor any amount
  of sorrow or pleasure can tear her out

of my heart—and what will become of me?
I'll keep on dying, unless I die really.
She'll never bring me any blessing,
only this pain that nothing can remedy,
  since neither sea nor land nor any amount
  of sorrow or pleasure can tear her out

of my heart. And what torments me the most,
I'll be honest, is knowing I'll suffer
whether I see her or whether I don't:
that's the greatest curse of a beloved
  whom neither sea nor land nor any amount
  of sorrow or pleasure can tear out.

90.

PAIO GOMES CHARINHO

cantiga de amor

Quantos hoj'andam eno mar aqui
coidam que coita no mundo nom há
senom do mar, nem ham outro mal já.
Mais doutra guisa contece hoje a mi:
  coita d'amor me faz escaecer
  a mui gram coita do mar e tẽer

pola maior coita de quantas som,
coita d'amor, a quen'a Deus quer dar.
E é gram coita de mort'a do mar,
mas nom é tal, e por esta razom
  coita d'amor me faz escaecer
  a mui gram coita do mar e tẽer

pola maior coita, per boa fé,
de quantas forom, nem som, nem serám.
E estes outros que amor nom ham
dizem que nom, mas eu direi qual é:
  coita d'amor me faz escaecer
  a mui gram coita d'amor e tẽer

por maior coita a que faz perder
coita do mar, que faz muitos morrer.

256

90.

PAIO GOMES CHARINHO

Song about the Pain of Love and Sea

Those who spend their lives at sea
think there is no pain in the world
as great as their pain, and no fate worse
than a seaman's fate, but consider me:
    the pain of love made me forget
    the pain of the sea, so harsh and yet

as nothing next to that greatest pain,
the pain of love that God ordains.
The pain of the sea is a pain unto death,
but I discovered it can't compare
    to the pain of love, which made me forget
    my seaman's pain, terrible and yet

as nothing next to the greatest of all
the pains that are, were, or will come.
Those who have never been in love
can't know the awful pain I feel—
    a pain that makes a man forget
    the pain of the sea, so harsh and yet

as nothing next to this pain that exceeds
even the pain of the deadly sea.

91.

PAIO GOMES CHARINHO

cantiga de amigo

As frores do meu amigo
briosas vam no navio,
   e vam-se as frores
   daqui bem com meus amores.
   Idas som as frores
   daqui bem com meus amores!

As frores do meu amado
briosas vam ẽno barco,
   e vam-se as frores
   daqui bem com meus amores.
   Idas som as frores
   daqui bem com meus amores!

Briosas vam no navio
pera chegar ao ferido,
   e vam-se as frores
   daqui bem com meus amores.
   Idas som as frores
   daqui bem com meus amores!

Briosas vam ẽno barco
pera chegar ao fossado,
   e vam-se as frores
   daqui bem com meus amores.
   Idas som as frores
   daqui bem com meus amores!

. . .

91.

PAIO GOMES CHARINHO

Song of the Parting Flowers

The flowers of my beloved
look splendid on the ship,
 and they're leaving now
 along with my love.
 Gone are the flowers
 along with my love!

The flowers of my friend
look splendid on the deck,
 and they're leaving now
 along with my love.
 Gone are the flowers
 along with my love!

Looking splendid on the ship,
they're headed off to battle,
 and they're leaving now
 along with my love.
 Gone are the flowers
 along with my love!

Looking splendid on the deck,
they're headed off to war,
 and they're leaving now
 along with my love!
 Gone are the flowers
 along with my love!

. . .

Pera chegar ao ferido
servir mi, corpo velido,
    e vam-se as frores
    daqui bem com meus amores.
    Idas som as frores
    daqui bem com meus amores!

Pera chegar ao fossado
servir mi, corpo loado,
    e vam-se as frores
    daqui bem com meus amores.
    Idas som as frores
    daqui bem com meus amores!

They're headed off to battle
to serve me, who am beautiful,
  and they're leaving now
  along with my love.
  Gone are the flowers
  along with my love!

They're headed off to war
to serve the girl he adores,
  and they're leaving now
  along with my love.
  Gone are the flowers
  along with my love!

92.

PAIO GOMES CHARINHO

cantiga de amigo

Disserom-m'hoj', ai amiga, que nom
é meu amig'almirante do mar,
e meu coraçom já pode folgar
e dormir já, e, por esta razom,
    o que do mar meu amigo sacou
    saque-o Deus de coitas, que ar jogou

mui bem a mim, ca já nom andarei
triste por vento que veja fazer,
nem por tormenta nom hei de perder
o sono, amiga; mais, se foi el-rei
    o que do mar meu amigo sacou,
    saque-o Deus de coitas, que ar jogou

mui bem a mim, ca, já cada que vir
algum home de fronteira chegar,
nom hei medo que mi diga pesar;
mais, porque m'el fez bem sem lho pedir,
    o que do mar meu amigo sacou
    saque-o Deus de coitas, que ar jogou

mui bem a mim.

92.

PAIO GOMES CHARINHO

Song about a Good Deed

Listen, Sister! They told me
my friend is an admiral of the sea
no longer. Now I can sleep
with a quiet heart. And so
    may the man who freed my friend from the sea
    be freed by God from sorrows, since to me

he did a good deed. Just think,
Sister! Now I won't worry
when the wind is high, and storms
won't rob me of sleep. If the king
    was the man who freed my friend from the sea,
    may God free him from sorrows, since to me

he did a good deed. My mind
need no longer fret each time
they announce the soldiers who've died.
For this unexpected kindness
    may the man who freed my friend from the sea
    be freed by God from sorrows, since to me

he did a good deed.

93.

PERO GONÇALVES DE PORTOCARREIRO

cantiga de amigo

Par Deus, coitada vivo,
pois nom vem meu amigo;
pois nom vem, que farei?
Meus cabelos, com sirgo
eu nom vos liarei.

Pois nom vem de Castela,
nom é viv', ai mesela,
ou mi o detém el-rei.
Mias toucas da Estela,
eu nom vos tragerei.

Pero m'eu leda semelho,
nom me sei dar conselho;
amigas, que farei?
Em vós, ai meu espelho,
eu nom me veerei.

Estas doas mui belas,
el mi as deu, ai donzelas,
nom vo-las negarei.
Mias cintas das fivelas,
eu nom vos cingerei.

93.

PERO GONÇALVES DE PORTOCARREIRO

Song for an Unreturned Lover

God knows how I hurt,
my lover's not here,
so now what will I do?
Silk ribbon for my hair,
you'll lie here unused.

He's still in Castile,
either dead—God help me!—
or detained by the king.
Bonnets from Estela,
I won't tie your strings.

Though I may look serene,
I'm confused, upset,
so now what, dear Sisters?
I'll gaze at myself
in this mirror no more.

These beautiful presents
are from him, dear friends,
I freely confess it.
For now, buckled belts,
you won't touch my waist.

94.

MARTIM MOXA

cantiga moral

Quem viu o mundo qual o eu já vi
e viu as gentes que eram entom
e viu aquestas que agora som,
Deus! Quand'i cuida, que pode cuidar?
Ca me sin'eu, per mim, quando cuid'i!
   Por que me nom vou algur esterrar,
   se poderia melhor mund'achar?

Mundo tẽemos fals'e sem sabor,
mundo sem Deus e em que bem nom há,
e mundo tal que nom corregerá,
ante o vejo sempr'empeorar.
Quand'est'eu cat'e vej'end'o melhor,
   por que me nom vou algur esterrar,
   se poderia melhor mund'achar?

U foi mesur'ou grãadez? U jaz
verdad'? U é quem há amigo leal?
Que fui d'amor ou trobar? Porque sal
a gente trist'e sol nom quer cantar?
Quand'est'eu cat'e quanto mal s'i faz,
   por que me nom vou algur esterrar,
   se poderia melhor mund'achar?

...

266

94.

MARTIM MOXA

Song about Why I Don't Go Away

Whoever has seen the world I've seen,
seen how people lived back then
and seen the way they are today—
thinking about it, what can he think?
Crossing myself, I think "God help us!"
        Why don't I just go away
        to find another, better world?

This world of ours is false and stale,
with no more God or goodness in it,
a world so broken it can't be fixed,
and I see it getting worse each day.
If I can imagine something different,
        why don't I just go away
        to find another, better world?

Where did grace and greatness flee?
Where truth and the truest friend?
What became of love and troubadours?
Why are we sad? Why don't we sing?
When I consider all these things,
        why don't I just go away
        to find another, better world?

. . .

Viv'eu em tal mund', e faz m'i viver
ũa dona, que quero mui gram bem,
e muit'há já que m'em seu poder tem,
bem dê'lo temp'u soíam amar.
Oimais, de mim pode quem quer saber
por que me nom vou algur esterrar,
se poderia melhor mund'achar.

Mais em tal mundo por que vai morar
home de prez, que s'en pod'alongar?

I live in such a world because
a lady I greatly love lives there.
I've been her slave since olden days,
back when love was still quite common.
This, if you want to know, explains
    why I don't just go away
        to find another, better world.

Why else would any man keep living
in such a world, if he could leave?

95.

JOAM AIRAS DE SANTIAGO

cantiga de amigo

Tôdalas cousas eu vejo partir
do mund', em como soíam seer,
e vej'as gentes partir de fazer
bem que soíam, tal tempo nos vem!
Mais nom se pod'o coraçom partir
do meu amigo de mi querer bem.

Pero que home part'o coraçom
das cousas que ama, per bõa fé,
e parte-s'home da terra ond'é,
e parte-s'home d'u grande prol tem,
nom se pode parti'lo coraçom
    do meu amigo de mi querer bem.

Tôdalas cousas eu vejo mudar,
mudam-s'os tempos e muda-s'o al,
muda-s'a gente em fazer bem ou mal,
mudam-s'os ventos e tod'outra rem,
mais nom se pod'o coraçom mudar
    do meu amigo de mi querer bem.

95.

JOAM AIRAS DE SANTIAGO

Song of Change

I see how everything is quitting
whatever it always was,
and I see people quitting what
they'd been for years—time is harsh!—
but my lover can never quit
loving me with his whole heart.

Although a man might turn his heart
away from things he's always loved,
or turn from lands where he has lived,
or even turn from his own well-being,
one thing's sure: my lover's heart
can't turn away from loving me.

I see how everything is changing:
seasons change all over the world,
people change for better or worse,
the winds and all things change with time.
But my lover can never change
what his heart feels for mine.

96.

JOAM AIRAS DE SANTIAGO

cantiga de amigo

Diz, amiga, o que mi gram bem quer
que nunca mais mi rem demandará,
sol que lh'ouça quanto dizer quiser,
e, mentre viver, que me servirá;
   e vedes ora com'é sabedor:
   que, pois que lh'eu tod'este bem fezer,
   log'el querrá que lhi faça melhor.

Mui bem cuid'eu que com mentira vem,
pero jura que mi nom quer mentir,
mais diz que fale conmig', e por en,
mentre viver, nom mi quer al pedir;
   e vedes ora com'é sabedor:
   que, pois que lh'eu tod'este bem fezer,
   log'el querrá que lhi faça melhor.

Gram pavor hei nom me queira enganar,
pero diz el que nom quer al de mim
senom falar mig', e mais demandar,
mentre viver, nom mi quer des ali;
   e vedes ora com'é sabedor:
   que, pois que lh'eu tod'este bem fezer,
   log'el querrá que lhi faça melhor.

E esto será mentr'o mundo for:
quant'home mais houver ou acabar,
tanto d'haver mais haverá sabor.

. . .

96.

JOAM AIRAS DE SANTIAGO

Song about a Man Who Wants to Talk

The man who is in love with me
says he'll never want anything
except to simply talk with me
and to serve me as long as he lives,
    but oh, is he ever clever!
    If I give in to his request,
    he'll press for something better.

I think he's lying through his teeth.
He claims he's honest to the core
and swears that all he'll ever seek
is to talk with me, nothing more,
    but oh, is he ever clever!
    If I give in to his request,
    he'll press for something better.

I'm deathly afraid of being deceived,
despite his ardent protestations
that in this life to talk with me
is his only aspiration,
    but oh, is he ever clever!
    If I give in to his request,
    he'll press for something better.

So it will be till the end of time:
however much a man receives,
that much more will he desire.

. . .

Mais id', amiga, vós, por meu amor,
conmig'ali u m'el quiser falar,
ca mal mi venha, se lh'eu soa for.

I beg you, Sister, to come along
to where he wants to have a talk,
because without you—that won't be all.

97.

JOAM AIRAS DE SANTIAGO

cantiga de amigo

Diz meu amigo tanto bem de mi
quant'el mais pod'e de meu parecer,
e os que sabem que o diz assi
têm que hei eu que lhi gradecer;
     em quant'el diz, nom lhi gradesc'eu rem,
     ca mi sei eu que mi paresco bem.

Diz-mi fremosa e diz-mi senhor,
e fremosa mi dirá quem me vir,
e têm que mi faz mui grand'amor
e que eu hei muito que lhi gracir;
     em quant'el diz, nom lhi gradesc'eu rem,
     ca mi sei eu que mi paresco bem.

Diz muito bem de mim em seu trobar
com gram dereit', e al vos en direi:
têm bem quantos me lh'oem loar
que eu muito que lhi gradecer hei;
     em quant'el diz, nom lhi gradesc'eu rem,
     ca mi sei eu que mi paresco bem.

Ca, se eu nom parecesse mui bem,
de quant'el diz non'o diria rem.

97.

JOAM AIRAS DE SANTIAGO

Song of One Who Knows She's Good-Looking

My beloved speaks very well of me,
praising my looks as much as he can,
and those who hear the words he speaks
think that I must owe him thanks,
    but I hear his praise and thank him for nothing;
    I know that I'm indeed good-looking.

He calls me "lady" and says I'm lovely
(as all who know me naturally say),
and thus, some think, he shows great love
for which I should, with thanks, repay,
    but I hear his praise and thank him for nothing;
    I know that I'm indeed good-looking.

He praises me in the songs he sings,
and rightly so, and I'll tell you more:
those who hear him praise me think
I have a lot to thank him for,
    but I hear his praise and thank him for nothing;
    I know that I'm indeed good-looking.

Because if I weren't indeed good-looking
he wouldn't praise me; he'd say nothing.

98.

JOAM AIRAS DE SANTIAGO

cantiga de amor

A mia senhor, que eu sei muit'amar,
punhei sempre do seu amor gaar
e non'o houvi; mais, a meu cuidar,
nom fui eu i de sem nem sabedor
por quanto lh'eu fui amor demandar,
  ca nunca vi molher mais sem amor.

E des que a vi sempr'a muit'amei,
e sempre lhi seu amor demandei,
e non'o houvi nen'o haverei;
mais se cent'anos for seu servidor,
nunca lh'eu já amor demandarei,
  ca nunca vi molher mais sem amor.

98.

JOAM AIRAS DE SANTIAGO

Song about a Loveless Lady

Because I greatly love my lady
I tried and tried, but always failed,
to win her love, having acted
out of passion, not with wisdom,
thinking she might love me back—
    I've never seen a more loveless woman.

Upon seeing her, I loved her madly
and sought her love but never had it
and never will. Were I to serve her
for a hundred more years, I wouldn't
ask again for any love in return—
    I've never seen a more loveless woman.

99.

JOAM AIRAS DE SANTIAGO

cantiga de amor

Com coitas d'amor, se Deus mi perdom,
trob', e dizem que meus cantares nom
valem rem, porque atam muitos som,
   mais muitas coitas mi os fazem fazer,
   e tantas coitas, quantas de sofrer
   hei, non'as posso em um cantar dizer.

Muitas hei, hei cuidad'e se mi sal,
e faço muitos cantares, em tal
que perça coitas, e dizem-mi mal,
   mais muitas coitas mi os fazem fazer,
   e tantas coitas, quantas de sofrer
   hei, non'as posso em um cantar dizer.

Em muitos cantares tenho que bem
posso dizer mias coitas, e por en
dizem-mi ora que faço i mal sem,
   mais muitas coitas mi os fazem fazer,
   e tantas coitas, quantas de sofrer
   hei, non'as posso em um cantar dizer.

Ca, se cuidar i, já mentre viver
bem cuido que as nom possa dizer.

99.

JOAM AIRAS DE SANTIAGO

Song about How I Make Songs

I make my songs, God forgive me,
with the pains of love, and I make so many
that some say they're not worth anything,
    but I feel pains of love so strong
    they can't all fit into just one song.

All the pains I have to express
go into songs, which help to lessen
the pain. Others question my method,
    but I feel pains of love so strong
    they can't all fit into just one song.

By making songs, as I've explained,
I can better tell my pains.
"You sing too much," some complain,
    but I feel pains of love so strong
    they can't all fit into just one song.

Thinking about the rest of my days,
I think I'll never tell all my pains.

100.

JOAM AIRAS DE SANTIAGO

pastorela

Pelo souto de Crexente
ũa pastor vi andar,
muit'alongada da gente,
alçando voz a cantar,
apertando-se na saia,
quando saía la raia
do sol, nas ribas do Sar.

E as aves que voavam,
quando saía l'alvor,
todas d'amores cantavam
pelos ramos d'arredor;
mais nom sei tal qu'i 'stevesse,
que em al cuidar podesse
senom todo em amor.

Ali 'stivi eu mui quedo,
quis falar e nom ousei,
empero dix'a gram medo:
—Mia senhor, falar-vos-ei
um pouco, se mi ascuitardes,
e ir-m'hei quando mandardes,
mais aqui nom estarei.

. . .

100.

JOAM AIRAS DE SANTIAGO

Pastoral Song

In the woods outside Crecente
I saw a shepherdess walking
apart from where others went,
and she raised her voice in song,
gathering the folds of her dress
as the sun began to break
over the banks of the Sar.

The birds flying around us
as the sun slowly rose
sang of love in unison
on branches high and low,
and I don't know a soul
who in that place and moment
would not have thought of love.

Wanting to speak but afraid,
for a long time I just watched,
and at last I timidly said:
"Madam, I'd like to talk
if you would kindly listen,
and when you wish, I'll leave,
I won't stay any longer."

. . .

—Senhor, por Santa Maria,
nom estedes mais aqui,
mais ide-vos vossa via,
faredes mesura i;
ca os que aqui chegarem,
pois que vos aqui acharem,
bem dirám que mais houv'i.

"Sir, by Blessed Mary,
don't stay another minute
but continue on your way,
showing respect for me,
for if anyone should appear
and see you with me here,
they'll say they saw much more."

101.

JOAM AIRAS DE SANTIAGO

cantiga de escárnio

Ũa dona, nom dig'eu qual,
nom aguirou ogano mal:
polas oitavas de Natal,
ia por sa missa oir,
e houv' um corvo carnaçal,
e nom quis da casa sair.

A dona, mui de coraçom,
oíra sa missa entom,
e foi por oír o sarmom,
e vedes que lho foi partir:
houve sig'um corv'a carom,
e nom quis da casa sair.

A dona disse: —Que será?
E i o clérig'está já
revestid'e maldizer-m'-á
se me na igreja nom vir.
E diss'o corvo: —Quá, cá;
e nom quis da casa sair.

Nunca taes agoiros vi
des aquel dia em que naci
com'aquest'ano houv'aqui;
e ela quis provar de s'ir
e houv'um corvo sobre si
e nom quis da casa sair.

101.

JOAM AIRAS DE SANTIAGO

Song about a Strange Omen

A woman whose name I'll save
took to heart an omen
received in the Christmas Octave:
on leaving for Mass she opened
her door to a carnivorous crow
    and decided to stay at home.

The pious woman sincerely
wished to hear Mass and hoped
to arrive in time for the sermon,
but look what kept her from going:
she found herself with a crow
    and decided to stay at home.

She said, "What will happen?
The priest has donned his robes
by now and will judge me badly
if at church I don't show."
"Caw, caw!" said the crow,
    and she decided to stay home.

Never since I was christened
have I ever seen such omens
as what occurred this Christmas:
she tried to go to the Holy
Mass but, charmed by a crow,
    decided to stay at home.

102.

JOAM AIRAS DE SANTIAGO

cantiga moral

Algum bem mi deve ced'a fazer
Deus, e fará-mi-o quando Lh'aprouguer.
Sempr'ando led'e quem mi falar quer
em pesar, nom lho posso padecer,
mais fuj'ant'el e nom lho quer'oir;
des i ar hei gram sabor de guarir
com quem sei que quer falar em prazer.

Ca todos andam cuidando em haver
e outra rem nom querem cuidar já,
e morrem ced'e fica tod'acá;
mais esto migo nom podem põer,
que trob'e cant'e cuido sempr'em bem,
e tenh'amiga que faz mui bom sem,
e pod'o tempo passar em prazer.

Nostro Senhor, que há mui gram poder,
é sempre ledo no seu coraçom,
e som mui ledos quantos com El som.
Por en faz mal, quant'é meu conhocer,
o que trist'é, que sempre cuida mal,
ca um pobre ledo mil tanto val
ca rico triste em que nom há prazer.

288

102.

JOAM AIRAS DE SANTIAGO

Song of a Contented Troubadour

Soon I'll be divinely favored,
whenever God bestows His grace.
Always content, I've little patience
for talking with those who only despair.
I turn my ear from their complaints,
preferring the wholesome conversation
of those who talk about life's pleasures.

People fret about material treasure,
shutting other things out of their mind,
and when they die, it all stays behind.
This way of living I could never accept.
I sing my poems, think of my blessings
and serve a lady full of good sense,
making the passing of time a pleasure.

The heart of Our Lord, a heart that's greater
than any other, is always content,
and content are all who in Him find rest.
That's why I think a man's in error
if he's glum and thinks the worst.
The poor contented man is worth
a thousand rich men who know no pleasure.

103.

JOAM ZORRO

cantiga de amor

Em Lixboa, sobre lo mar,
barcas novas mandei lavrar,
ai mia senhor veelida!

Em Lixboa, sobre lo lez,
barcas novas mandei fazer,
ai mia senhor veelida!

Barcas novas mandei lavrar
e no mar as mandei deitar,
ai mia senhor veelida!

Barcas novas mandei fazer
e no mar as mandei meter,
ai mia senhor veelida!

103.

JOAM ZORRO

Song of New Ships

On Lisbon's beach
I built new boats,
   oh lovely lady!

On Lisbon's shore
I built new ships,
   oh lovely lady!

I built new boats
and set them afloat,
   oh lovely lady!

I built new ships
and put them to sea,
   oh lovely lady!

104.

JOAM ZORRO

cantiga de amigo

El-rei de Portugale
barcas mandou lavrare,
   e lá irá nas barcas sigo,
   mia filha, o voss'amigo.

El-rei portugueese
barcas mandou fazere,
   e lá irá nas barcas sigo,
   mia filha, o voss'amigo.

Barcas mandou lavrare
e no mar as deitare,
   e lá irá nas barcas sigo,
   mia filha, o voss'amigo.

Barcas mandou fazere
e no mar as metere,
   e lá irá nas barcas sigo,
   mia filha, o voss'amigo.

104.

JOAM ZORRO

Song about the King's Boats

The king of Portugal
ordered boats made,
    and with him in those boats
    your friend, dear Daughter, will sail.

The Portuguese king
ordered boats built,
    and with him in those boats
    your friend, dear Daughter, will sail.

He ordered boats made
and launched into the water,
    and with him in those boats
    your friend, dear Daughter, will sail.

He ordered boats built
and launched into the sea,
    and with him in those boats
    your friend, dear Daughter, will sail.

105.

JOAM ZORRO

cantiga de amigo

Jus'a lo mar e o rio
   eu namorada irei,
u el-rei arma navio:
   amores, convosco m'irei.

Juso a lo mar e o alto
   eu namorada irei,
u el-rei arma o barco:
   amores, convosco m'irei.

U el-rei arma navio
   (eu namorada irei)
pera levar a virgo:
   amores, convosco m'irei.

U el-rei arma o barco
   (eu namorada irei)
pera levar a d'algo:
   amores, convosco m'irei.

105.

JOAM ZORRO

Song of a Girl Going Down to the River

Down to the river and the sea
    I, so in love, will go.
Where the king is outfitting a ship:
    with you, my love, I'll go.

Down to the river and the ocean
    I, so in love, will go.
Where the king is outfitting a boat:
    with you, my love, I'll go.

Where the king is outfitting a ship
    (I, so in love, will go)
to carry on board a young girl:
    with you, my love, I'll go.

Where the king is outfitting a boat
    (I, so in love, will go)
to carry a girl who's noble:
    with you, my love, I'll go.

106.

JOAM ZORRO

cantiga de amigo

—Cabelos, los meus cabelos,
el-rei m'enviou por elos!
    Ai madre, que lhis farei?
—Filha, dade-os a el-rei.

—Garcetas, las mias garcetas,
el-rei m'enviou por elas!
    Ai madre, que lhis farei?
—Filha, dade-as a el-rei.

106.

JOAM ZORRO

Song about a Request for Hair

—Mother, the king has declared
that he wants my hair. My hair!
What shall I do?
—Give it, Daughter, to the king.

—Mother, the king has said
he wants my braids. My braids!
What shall I do?
—Give them, Daughter, to the king.

107.

JOAM ZORRO

cantiga de amigo

Pela ribeira do rio salido
trebelhei, madre, com meu amigo.
Amor hei migo,
que nom houvesse;
fiz por amig'o
que nom fezesse.

Pela ribeira do rio levado
trebelhei, madre, com meu amado.
Amor hei migo,
que nom houvesse;
fiz por amig'o
que nom fezesse.

107.

JOAM ZORRO

Song of What I Wish I Hadn't Done

I went to the shore of the surging river
to frolic, Mother, with my beloved.
    I wish I didn't feel
    this feeling of love!
    With my friend I did
    what I wish I hadn't done!

To the shore of the surging river I went
to frolic, Mother, with my friend.
    I wish I didn't feel
    this feeling of love!
    With my friend I did
    what I wish I hadn't done!

108.

DINIS, KING OF PORTUGAL

cantiga de amigo

Levantou-s'a velida,
    levantou-s'alva,
e vai lavar camisas
    eno alto,
    vai-las lavar alva.

Levantou-s'a louçana,
    levantou-s'alva,
e vai lavar delgadas
    eno alto,
    vai-las lavar alva.

E vai lavar camisas,
    levantou-s'alva;
o vento lhas desvia
    eno alto,
    vai-las lavar alva.

E vai lavar delgadas,
    levantou-s'alva;
o vento lhas levava
    eno alto,
    vai-las lavar alva.

O vento lhas desvia,
    levantou-s'alva;
meteu-s'a alva em ira
    eno alto,
    vai-las lavar alva.

108.

Song about a Girl Washing Shirts

> She wakes up lovely
>   by the light of dawn
> and goes to wash shirts
>   in the stream.
>   White as the dawn she goes.
>
> She wakes up pretty
>   by the light of dawn
> and washes chemises
>   in the stream.
>   White as the dawn she goes.
>
> She goes to wash shirts
>   by the light of dawn;
> they're strewn by the wind
>   in the stream.
>   White as the dawn she goes.
>
> She washes chemises
>   by the light of dawn;
> they're strewn by the breeze
>   in the stream.
>   White as the dawn she goes.
>
> They're strewn by the wind
>   by the light of dawn;
> she becomes livid
>   at the stream.
>   White as the dawn she goes.

O vento lhas levava,
    levantou-s'alva;
meteu-s'a alva em sanha
    eno alto,
    vai-las lavar alva.

They're strewn by the breeze
    by the light of dawn;
she blanches with fury
    at the stream.
      White as the dawn she goes.

109.

DINIS, KING OF PORTUGAL

cantiga de amigo

—Ai flores, ai flores do verde pino,
se sabedes novas do meu amigo?
   Ai Deus, e u é?

Ai flores, ai flores do verde ramo,
se sabedes novas do meu amado?
   Ai Deus, e u é?

Se sabedes novas do meu amigo,
aquel que mentiu do que pôs conmigo?
   Ai Deus, e u é?

Se sabedes novas do meu amado,
aquel que mentiu do que mi há jurado?
   Ai Deus, e u é?

—Vós me preguntades polo voss'amigo
e eu bem vos digo que é san'e vivo.
   —Ai Deus, e u é?

—Vós me preguntades polo voss'amado
e eu bem vos digo que é viv'e sano.
   —Ai Deus, e u é?

—E eu bem vos digo que é san'e vivo
e será vosco ant'o prazo saído.
   —Ai Deus, e u é?

. . .

109.

Song of the Flowers of the Green Pine

Flowers of the green pine, oh flowers,
do you have news of my lover?
   Oh God, and where is he?

Oh flowers, flowers of the green branch,
do you have news of my friend?
   Oh God, and where is he?

Do you have news of my lover,
who has proved himself a liar?
   Oh God, and where is he?

Do you have news of my friend,
who did not come when he said?
   Oh God, and where is he?

You ask me about your friend,
and I tell you he's alive and well.
   Oh God, and where is he?

You ask me about your lover,
and I tell you he's well, he's alive.
   Oh God, and where is he?

I tell you he's alive and well
and will be with you in a while.
   Oh God, and where is he?

. . .

—E eu bem vos digo que é viv'e sano
e será vosco ant'o prazo passado.
　—Ai Deus, e u é?

I tell you he's well, he's alive,
and will come by the appointed time.
Oh God, and where is he?

110.

cantiga de amigo

De que morredes, filha, a do corpo velido?
—Madre, moiro d'amores que mi deu meu amigo.
Alva é, vai liero.

—De que morredes, filha, a do corpo louçano?
-—Madre, moiro d'amores que mi deu meu amado.
Alva é, vai liero.

Madre, moiro d'amores que mi deu meu amigo,
quando vej'esta cinta que por seu amor cingo.
Alva é, vai liero.

Madre, moiro d'amores que mi deu meu amado,
quando vej'esta cinta que por seu amor trago.
Alva é, vai liero.

Quando vej'esta cinta que por seu amor cingo
e me nembra, fremosa, como falou conmigo.
Alva é, vai liero.

Quando vej'esta cinta que por seu amor trago
e me nembra, fremosa, como falámos ambos.
Alva é, vai liero.

110.

DINIS, KING OF PORTUGAL

Song of a Girl Dying of Loves

What are you dying of, Daughter so pretty?
I die of loves, Mother, that my friend gave to me.
It's dawn, and he's gone!

What are you dying of, Daughter so lovely?
I die of loves, Mother, received from my beloved.
It's dawn, and he's gone!

I die of loves, Mother, that my friend gave to me,
when I see this belt that for his love I'm wearing.
It's dawn, and he's gone!

I die of loves, Mother, received from my beloved,
when I see this belt that I wear for his love.
It's dawn, and he's gone!

When I see this belt that for his love I'm wearing
I remember, who am fair, how he talked with me.
It's dawn, and he's gone!

When I see this belt that I wear for his love
I remember, who am fair, how we talked with each other.
It's dawn, and he's gone!

111.

DINIS, KING OF PORTUGAL

cantiga de amor

—Em grave dia, senhor, que vos oí
falar, e vos virom estes olhos meus.
—Dized', amigo, que poss'eu fazer i
em aqueste feito, se vos valha Deus?
—Faredes mesura contra mi, senhor?
—Farei, amigo, fazend'eu o melhor.

—U vos em tal ponto eu oí falar,
senhor, que nom pudi depois bem haver.
—Amigo, quero-vos ora preguntar
que mi digades o que poss'i fazer.
—Faredes mesura contra mi, senhor?
—Farei, amigo, fazend'eu o melhor.

—Des que vos vi e vos oí falar, nom
vi prazer, senhor, nem dormi, nem folguei.
—Amigo, dizede, se Deus vos perdom,
o que eu i faça, ca eu non'o sei.
—Faredes mesura contra mi, senhor?
—Farei, amigo, fazend'eu o melhor.

111.

DINIS, KING OF PORTUGAL

Song of a Lover Asking a Favor

—On a fateful day, dear lady, I heard
you speak and first laid eyes on you.
—*Tell me, friend, in this regard,*
what by God's grace I can do.
    —Will you treat me kindly, lady?
    —*I will, my friend, by doing what's best.*

—Ever since I heard you speak,
dear lady, I've known only grief.
—*Friend, I'd like to know what you seek*
from me that might bring some relief.
    —Will you treat me kindly, lady?
    —*I will, my friend, by doing what's best.*

—To see and hear you speak, dear lady,
took pleasure, peace, and sleep from me.
—*So tell me, friend, God allowing,*
what I can do, as I've no idea.
    —Will you treat me kindly, lady?
    —*I will, my friend, by doing what's best.*

112.

DINIS, KING OF PORTUGAL

cantiga de escárnio

U noutro dia seve Dom Foam
a mi começou gram noj'a crecer
de muitas cousas que lh'oí dizer.
Diss'el: —Ir-m'-ei ca já se deitar ham.
E dix'eu: —Bõa ventura hajades,
porque vos ides e me leixades.

E muit'enfadado de seu parlar
sevi gram peça, se mi valha Deus,
e tosquiavam estes olhos meus.
E quand'el disse: —Ir-me quer'eu deitar,
lhe dix'eu: —Bõa ventura hajades,
porque vos ides e me leixades.

El seve muit'e diss'e parfiou
e a mim creceu gram nojo por en
e nom soub'el se x'era mal se bem.
E quand'el disse: —Já m'eu deitar vou,
dixi-lh'eu: —Bõa ventura hajades,
porque vos ides e me leixades.

112.

DINIS, KING OF PORTUGAL

Song about a Mr. So-and-So

Mr. So-and-So, the other evening,
talked so much I thought he'd keep me
up all night, till finally he said,
"I'm going home, it's time for bed,"
    and I said, "I wish you all the best,
    since you're leaving and I can rest."

I got so sick of having to listen
to him go on—God be my witness—
I couldn't keep my eyelids open,
and when he said, "I'm going home,"
    I said, "I wish you all the best,
    since you're leaving and I can rest."

He chattered on for the longest time,
until he'd bored me out of my mind,
not caring what I might have to say,
and when he said, "I'll be on my way,"
    I said, "I wish you all the best,
    since you're leaving and I can rest."

113.

DINIS, KING OF PORTUGAL

cantiga de amor

Quer'eu em maneira de proençal
fazer agora um cantar d'amor
e querrei muit'i loar mia senhor
a que prez nem fremosura nom fal,
nem bondade, e mais vos direi en:
tanto a fez Deus comprida de bem
que mais que todas las do mundo val.

Ca mia senhor quiso Deus fazer tal,
quando a fez, que a fez sabedor
de todo bem e de mui gram valor,
e com tod'esto é mui comunal
ali u deve; er deu-lhi bom sem
e des i nom lhi fez pouco de bem
quando nom quis que lh'outra foss'igual.

Ca em mia senhor nunca Deus pôs mal,
mais pôs i prez e beldad'e loor
e falar mui bem e riir melhor
que outra molher; des i é leal
muit'; e por esto nom sei hoj'eu quem
possa compridamente no seu bem
falar, ca nom há, tra'lo seu bem, al.

113.

Song in Provençal Style

In Provençal style I'd like
to make a song of love
to greatly praise my lady,
who's virtuous, good-looking
and kind. God granted her
more virtue than He did other
women of whatever land.

Wanting her to excel,
God created my lady
to be talented and worthy
yet also cordial, simple,
full of common sense
and every virtue; hence
no lady could be her equal.

Placing in her no error,
God made my lady beautiful,
clever, well-spoken, and cheerful
like no other woman, and very
loyal. I don't know who
could fully tell her virtues,
as she's past all compare.

114.

cantiga de amor

Proençaes soem mui bem trobar
e dizem eles que é com amor,
mais os que trobam no tempo da flor
e nom em outro, sei eu bem que nom
ham tam gram coita no seu coraçom
qual m'eu por mia senhor vejo levar.

Pero que trobam e sabem loar
sas senhores o mais e o melhor
que eles podem, sõo sabedor
que os que trobam quand'a frol sazom
há e nom ante, se Deus mi perdom,
nom ham tal coita qual eu hei sem par.

Ca os que trobam e que s'alegrar
vam eno tempo que tem a color
a frol consig'e, tanto que se for
aquel tempo, log'em trobar razom
nom ham, nem vivem em qual perdiçom
hoj'eu vivo, que pois m'há de matar.

114.

Song about the Provençal Poets

The Provençal poets sing well,
and they say they do it with love,
but poets who compose songs
only in the time of flowers
don't know the kind of suffering
my heart endures for my lady.

Although they praise their ladies
as well as they can in the songs
they compose, I know very well
that those who sing only in spring
know not, God forgive me,
the suffering my heart feels.

Those who rejoice and make poems
when the flower is full with color
and, once the season is over,
forget their calling as poets
don't know the hell I am living,
this love that's sure to kill me.

115.

cantiga de amor

Um tal home sei eu, ai bem talhada,
que por vós ten'a sa morte chegada
Veedes quem é, seed'en nembrada:
eu, mia dona.

Um tal home sei eu que preto sente
de si a morte chegada certamente.
Veedes quem é, venha-vos em mente:
eu, mia dona.

Um tal home sei eu, aquest'oíde,
que por vós morre, vó'lo en partide.
Veedes quem é, nom xe vos obride:
eu, mia dona.

115.

Song about a Man I Know

I know a man, oh beloved so fair,
whose death, because of you, is near.
Open your eyes so as to remember
   me, dear lady.

I know a man whose fate is decided,
whose death is doubtless close by.
Open your eyes and recall to mind
   me, dear lady.

I know a man—hear me yet!—
whose death only you can prevent.
Open your eyes so as not to forget
   me, dear lady.

116.

cantiga de amor

Senhor fremosa, vejo-vos queixar
porque vos am', e no meu coraçom
hei mui gram pesar, se Deus mi perdom,
porque vej'end'a vós haver pesar,
e queria-m'en de grado quitar,
mais nom posso forçar o coraçom,

que mi forçou meu saber e meu sem,
des i meteu-me no vosso poder.
E do pesar que vos eu vej'haver,
par Deus, senhor, a mim pesa muit'en,
e partir-m'-ia de vos querer bem,
mais tolhe-m'end'o coraçom poder,

que me forçou de tal guisa, senhor,
que sem nem força nom hei já de mi.
E do pesar que vós tomades i,
tom'eu pesar, que nom posso maior,
e queria nom vos haver amor,
mais o coraçom pode mais ca mi.

116.

DINIS, KING OF PORTUGAL

Song for a Vexed Lady

Fair lady, I know you complain
of my love, and in my heart
it vexes me to be vexing
you, by God. For my part
I'd gladly renounce my affection,
but I can't force this heart,

which forced out sense and reason
and threw me into your power.
The vexation you feel, God knows,
fills me with a vexing sorrow,
and I'd quit this love tomorrow
if I could, but I'm ruled by a power

that forced me, my lady, to give up
my sense and my will. If I
could cure your vexation, I'd relieve
my own, but it's useless to try.
I'd love to end this love,
but my heart is stronger than I.

117.

cantiga de amor

Nostro Senhor, hajades bom grado
por quanto m'hoje mia senhor falou,
e tod'esto foi porque se cuidou
que andava doutra namorado,
    ca sei eu bem que mi nom falara,
    se de qual bem lh'eu quero cuidara.

Porque mi falou hoj'este dia,
hajades bom grado, Nostro Senhor,
e tod'esto foi porque mia senhor
cuidou que eu por outra morria,
    ca sei eu bem que mi nom falara,
    se de qual bem lh'eu quero cuidara.

Porque m'hoje falou, haja Deus
bom grado, mais desto nom fora rem
senom porque mia senhor cuidou bem
que doutra eram os desejos meus,
    ca sei eu bem que mi nom falara,
    se de qual bem lh'eu quero cuidara.

Ca tal é que ante se matara
ca mi falar, se o sol cuidara.

117.

DINIS, KING OF PORTUGAL
Song of a Thankful Troubadour

Today I give thee thanks, O Lord,
for the long while my lady talked
with me—and all because she thought
that I'm in love with another lady,
  as I know she'd never talk with me
  had she any idea how I long for her.

Because she talked with me today
my thanks, O Lord, I give to thee
—and all because my lady believes
I'm dying of love for another lady,
  as I know she'd never talk with me
  had she any idea how I long for her.

She talked with me for a long time,
and I give thee thanks, O Lord, for this,
although it was only because she thinks
that another lady must be mine,
  as I know she'd never talk with me
  had she any idea how I long for her.

In fact, she'd rather commit suicide
than talk with me, had she any idea.

118.

pastorela

Ũa pastor bem talhada
cuidava em seu amigo
e estava, bem vos digo,
per quant'eu vi, mui coitada,
e diss': "Oimais nom é nada
de fiar per namorado
nunca molher namorada,
pois que mi o meu há errado".

Ela tragia na mão
um papagai mui fremoso,
cantando mui saboroso,
ca entrava o verão,
e diss': "Amigo loução,
que faria per amores?
Pois m'errastes tam em vão!"
E caeu antr'ũas flores.

Ũa gram peça do dia
jouv'ali, que nom falava,
e a vezes acordava
e a vezes esmorecia,
e diss': "Ai Santa Maria!
que será de mim agora?"
E o papagai dizia:
"Bem, per quant'eu sei, senhora".

. . .

118.

Pastoral Song

A pretty shepherd girl
was musing on her lover,
and I could tell by looking
that she was feeling grieved,
and she said, "Never again
should a girl in love believe
whatever her lover claims,
since by mine I was deceived."

In her hand she carried
a bright and beautiful parrot,
whose singing was quite pleasant,
for spring was in the air,
and she said, "Handsome lover,
who stupidly failed to appear,
what shall I do with my love?"
And she fell into some flowers.

For a good part of the day
she lay there without a word,
and sometimes she would stir,
and sometimes she would faint,
and she said, "Holy Mary,
what will become of me now?"
And the parrot answered, "Lady,
you'll prosper, as far as I know."

. . .

"Se me queres dar guarida",
diss'a pastor, "di verdade,
papagai, por caridade,
ca morte m'é esta vida".
Disse el: "Senhor comprida
de bem, e nom vos queixedes,
ca o que vos há servida,
erged'olho e vee-lo-edes".

"If you wish to help me,
parrot, for goodness' sake
be honest," the shepherdess said,
"for this life to me is death."
And he said, "Don't complain,
lady full of virtues,
but lift your eyes instead
to see the one who serves you."

119.

FERNANDO ESQUIO

cantiga de amigo

Vaiamos, irmana, vaiamos dormir
nas ribas do lago u eu andar vi
a las aves meu amigo.

Vaiamos, irmana, vaiamos folgar
nas ribas do lago u eu vi andar
a las aves meu amigo.

Nas ribas do lago u eu andar vi,
seu arco na mãao as aves ferir,
a las aves meu amigo.

Nas ribas do lago u eu vi andar,
seu arco na mãao a las aves tirar,
a las aves meu amigo.

Seu arco na mano as aves ferir
e las que cantavam leixa-las guarir,
a las aves meu amigo.

Seu arco na mano a las aves tirar
e las que cantavam non'as quer matar,
a las aves meu amigo.

119.

FERNANDO ESQUIO

Song about a Lover Who Hunts

Come with me, Sister, let's go sleep
alongside the lake where I have seen
   my lover hunting birds.

Come with me, Sister, let's rest awhile
alongside the lake where I have watched
   my lover hunting birds.

Alongside the lake where I have seen
his bow in hand and shot birds falling,
   my lover hunting birds.

Alongside the lake where I have watched
his bow, his arrows, and the birds that fall,
   my lover hunting birds.

His bow in hand and shot birds falling,
but he lets the ones that sing keep living,
   my lover hunting birds.

His bow, his arrows, and the birds that fall,
but those that sing he doesn't kill,
   my lover hunting birds.

120.

FERNANDO ESQUIO

cantiga de escárnio

A um frade dizem escaralhado,
e faz pecado quem lho vai dizer,
ca, pois el sabe arreitar de foder,
cuid'eu que gai é, de piss'arreitado;
e pois emprenha estas com que jaz
e faze filhos e filhas assaz,
ante lhe dig'eu bem encaralhado.

Escaralhado nunca eu diria,
mais que traje ante caralho ou veite,
ao que tantas molheres de leite
tem, ca lhe parirom três em um dia,
e outras muitas prenhadas que tem;
e atal frade cuid'eu que mui bem
encaralhado per esto seria.

Escaralhado nom pode seer
o que tantas filhas fez em Marinha
e que tem ora outra pastorinha
prenhe, que ora quer encaecer,
e outras muitas molheres que fode;
e atal frade bem cuid'eu que pode
encaralhado per esto seer.

120.

FERNANDO ESQUIO

Song about a Friar Said to be Impotent

A friar they say is impotent
really doesn't fit the case,
since he cheerfully fornicates
with a cock undeniably competent.
He gets the girls he lies with pregnant,
making sons and daughters aplenty,
so I would say he's well equipped.

Instead of "impotent" I would say
his cock is stiff and ready to fuck.
Just look at his women giving suck:
three gave birth on the same day,
and he's got others now expecting.
And so the friar, by my reckoning,
is well equipped, with power to stay.

"Impotent" is not the word
for one who's sired so many children
with Marinha, and now a different
girl he's fucking will soon give birth,
and there are many others he fucks.
I'm sure that such a friar must
be equipped with a cock that works.

121.

ESTEVAM COELHO

cantiga de amigo

Sedia la fremosa seu sirgo torcendo,
sa voz manselinha fremoso dizendo
cantigas d'amigo.

Sedia la fremosa seu sirgo lavrando,
sa voz manselinha fremoso cantando
cantigas d'amigo.

—Par Deus de cruz, dona, sei eu que havedes
amor mui coitado, que tam bem dizedes
cantigas d'amigo.

Par Deus de cruz, dona, sei eu que andades
d'amor mui coitada, que tam bem cantades
cantigas d'amigo.

—Avuitor comestes, que adevinhades!

121.

ESTEVAM COELHO

Song about a Girl Twisting Silk

While twisting silk a lovely girl
in a soft and lovely voice was singing
    songs of love.

While twisting silk a lovely young woman
in a soft and lovely voice was humming
    songs of love.

*—By God on the Cross, lady, I think
there's someone for whom you so well sing
    these songs of love.*

*By God on the Cross, lady, there must
be someone for whom you so well hum
    these songs of love.*

—You vulture eater, you guessed the truth!

122.

cantiga de amigo

Se hoj'o meu amigo
soubess', iria migo:
    eu al rio me vou banhar,
    e al mar.

Se hoj'el este dia
soubesse, migo iria:
    eu al rio me vou banhar,
    e al mar.

Quem lhi dissess'atanto:
ca já filhei o manto;
    eu al rio me vou banhar,
    e al mar.

122.

ESTEVAM COELHO

Song of a Girl Going to Bathe

If my friend only knew,
today he'd go too:
    I'm off to the river to bathe,
    by the sea.

If he only knew where,
he'd go with me there:
    I'm off to the river to bathe,
    by the sea.

My cape's on my shoulders;
if only they'd told him:
    I'm off to the river to bathe,
    by the sea.

123.

VIDAL

cantiga de amor

Faz-m'agora por si morrer e traz-me mui coitado
mia senhor do bom parecer e do cós bem talhado,
a por que hei morte a prender come cervo lançado,
que se vai do mund'a perder da companha das cervas.
E mal dia nom ensandeci e pasesse das ervas
e nom viss', u primeiro vi, a mui fremosinha d'Elvas.

Oimais a morrer me convém, ca tam coitado sejo
pola mia senhor do bom sem, que am'e que desejo,
e que me parec'er tam bem cada que a eu vejo,
que semelha rosa que vem quando sal d'antr'as relvas.
E mal dia nom ensandeci e pasesse das ervas
e nom viss', u primeiro vi, a mui fremosinha d'Elvas.

123.

VIDAL

Song about a Lady from Elvas

My lady's making me perish
from a heart-tormenting passion
aroused by her lovely presence,
her figure so finely fashioned.
It's her fault I'm facing death,
like a wounded stag that abandons
the company of does he relished
in the world he's leaving forever.
>   If only that day I'd been
>   deranged or under a spell
>   and thus had never seen
>   my lovely lady from Elvas!

Let my death come soon:
I'm weary of always suffering
for that worthy lady whom
I cherish and love sincerely.
So splendid is her beauty
that every time I see her
I think of roses blooming
amid the grassy dells.
>   If only that day I'd been
>   deranged or under a spell
>   and thus had never seen
>   my lovely lady from Elvas!

124.

AFONSO SANCHES AND VASCO MARTINS
DE RESENDE

tençõo

—Vaasco Martins, pois vós trabalhades
e trabalhastes de trobar d'amor,
do que agora, par Nostro Senhor,
quero saber de vós, que mi o digades,
dizede-mi-o, ca bem vos estará:
pois vos esta, por que trobastes, já
morreu, par Deus, senhor, por quem trobades?

—Afonso Sanches, vós me preguntades
e quero-vos eu fazer sabedor:
eu trobo e trobei pola melhor
das que Deus fez, esto ben'o creades.
Esta do coraçom nom me salrá,
e atenderei seu bem, se mi o fará;
e vós al de mim saber nom queirades.

—Vaasco Martins, vós nom respondedes,
nem er entendo, assi veja prazer,
por que trobades, que ouvi dizer
que aquela por que trobad'havedes,
e que amastes vós mais doutra rem,
que vos morreu há gram temp', e por en
pola morta a trobar nom devedes.

—Afonso Sanches, pois nom entendedes
em qual guisa vos eu fui responder,
a mim en culpa nom devem poer,
mais a vós, se o saber nom podedes.

338

124.

AFONSO SANCHES AND VASCO MARTINS
DE RESENDE

Song about a Living Dead Lady

—Vasco Martins, you who strive
as much as ever to compose your songs
of love, I'd like to know by God
(if you don't mind my asking) why
you still compose them, seeing as the lady
for whom you sang and sing is dead?

—Afonso Sanches, since you ask,
I'll try my best to tell you why.
My singing was and is for the finest
of God's creatures, be sure of that.
Know that in my heart she reigns
and I still hope to win her favor.

—Vasco Martins, you haven't answered
and I don't understand, so tell me,
please, why your songs still celebrate
this lady of whom you were so enamored
but who they say has already died,
making your songs most ill advised.

—Afonso Sanches, if you don't grasp
my meaning, the fault is yours, not mine,
for in this matter of love you're blind.
I sing for one who in beauty surpasses
the rest, who has me under her sway,
and who is alive and not as you say.

Eu trobo pola que m'em poder tem
e vence todas de parecer bem,
pois viva é, ca nom como dizedes.

—Vaasco Martins, pois morreu por quem
sempre trobastes, maravilho-m'en,
pois vos morreu, como nom morredes.

—Afonso Sanches, vós sabede bem
que viva é e comprida de sem
a por que eu trob', e sabê-lo-edes.

—Vasco Martins, since the lady
for whom you've always sung is dead,
I marvel that you don't likewise die.

—*Afonso Sanches, be well aware*
I sing for a lady beyond compare,
a lady most wise and very alive.

NOTES TO THE POEMS

3 Montemaior probably refers to Montemor-o-Velho, an ancient fortified town west of Coimbra. There, in 1223, a peace treaty was signed between the new Portuguese king, Sancho II, and his aunts, who were sisters of the previous king. Gil Sanches, their half brother, may have written this cantiga in that same year.

4 The refrain is reproduced here as it appears in the cancioneiros. Rip Cohen, however, argues that the three middle lines of the refrain were probably meant to be one long line with inner rhyme.

6 The third and fourth lines of the second stanza literally read "and concerning whom God made him see things that caused him to die of grief."

7 Scholars are in doubt about the correct wording for several lines in this cantiga, and interpretations also vary. The attitude of the troubadour is clearly ironic, which is sometimes the case in cantigas de amor, but to name one's lady violates the code of fin'amor, so that this song could also be classified as a cantiga de escárnio.

9 In another cantiga poking fun at Lopo, Martim Soares reports that listeners would give the jongleur money or a present to be spared his playing the *citola*, a kind of lute, and then a further remuneration so that he would quit singing.

12 Attributed to Afonso Anes do Cotom in the *Cancioneiro da Vaticana* but to Pero Viviães in the *Cancioneiro da Biblioteca Nacional*. The copyist of the latter songbook is usually more reliable. The ribald theme, however, is typical of Anes do Cotom, who wrote another cantiga about the soldadeira (see the introduction)

Marinha Sabugal, probably the same Marinha mentioned in the cantiga translated here.

References to a "first sleep" (line 11) can be found in other writings during the following centuries, up until Dickens's *Barnaby Rudge*. Anthropological research has shown that many people's sleep used to be segmented, with activities such as conversation, sex, and even physical work taking place between the first and second sleeps.

13 This cantiga is reminiscent of the Occitan *alba*, in which two secret lovers must separate at sunrise.

16 Note the use of the technique called *mozdobre*, whereby end words are repeated but in different inflections.

17 Maria Perez Balteira was a soldadeira (see the introduction), singing and dancing for money in the courtly circuit. Perez Balteira's sexual promiscuity gave rise to satiric cantigas by half a dozen troubadours.

18 Garcia López de Alfaro was a cleric from the nobility who worked as a diplomat for the monarchs of Navarre, helping to settle disputes with the Castilian kings Ferdinand III and Alfonso X. The stinginess of noblemen was a popular theme of satire, but it's possible that this cantiga was mocking a lopsided political proposal made by López de Alfaro in his role as a negotiator.

20 As the headnote to this cantiga in the cancioneiros indicates, the lampoon is aimed not only at Martim Marcos (about whom nothing is known) but also at Don Manuel, the younger brother of Alfonso X and the "other lord" whom Villainy will seek as a home, according to the second stanza.

31 The daughter of a nobleman attached to the court of Portugal's King Sancho I, Guiomar Afonso Gata was one of the mistresses of King Afonso III. Both this and the following song by Roi Queimado are atypical cantigas de amor, in part because they

name the beloved woman, and they could be classified as cantigas de escárnio.

35 Maria Negra was no doubt a performing artist (a soldadeira; see introduction) who worked in collaboration with troubadours. The crude humor of this cantiga turns on the verb *sorrabar*, in the refrain, which means "to fawn on, flatter, pursue." The verb derives from *so* (under) + *rabo* (buttocks), making it effectively the equivalent, in modern English, of "to brownnose" or "to kiss ass."

36 Here the troubadour uses the vocabulary of equine pathology to make fun of Maria Negra's alleged sexual voraciousness.

37 Various troubadours mocked the homosexual activities of Fernando (Fernam) Diaz, about whom nothing is known except what can be gleaned from a few cantigas. As a *meirinho* (translated here as "sheriff"), he would have been responsible for keeping law and order, settling legal disputes, and looking out for the king's interests, which often had to compete with those of powerful nobles. Viveiro is a coastal town north of La Coruña; Carrión lies between León and Burgos. The key to understanding this cantiga is a phrase occurring in the first and second stanzas, *vai sobr'el*, which can mean "he goes after him" but also "he gets on top of him." In stanza 3, *fez sobr'el* is similarly ambiguous.

39 Fernando Escalho, a singer and reputed sodomite, was alluded to in cantigas by two other troubadours, Roi Pais de Ribela and Pero Garcia de Ambroa.

42 This is the best Galician-Portuguese example of the *descort*, an Occitan genre in which the strophes varied in length, meter, rhyme, and melody, so as to reflect the "discordant" psychological or emotional state of the troubadour.

44 Joam Soares Coelho had composed a cantiga de amor for a nursemaid, who was probably part of the royal retinue and had the status of a noblewoman, but the word "nursemaid" was enough to

provoke laughter and a storm of satiric responses from fellow troubadours.

46 The second line of the refrain translates literally as "the light would now be with me," suggesting that the narrator's lover is a source of light in her life.

48 For most of the twentieth century the majority of scholars thought that the words of this cantiga's refrain (lines 2 and 4 of each stanza) were gibberish, important only for their musical sound. Rip Cohen and Federico Corriente have proposed that the words *lelia doura* are a phonetic representation of Andalusian Arabic *líya ddáwa*, meaning "to me [belongs] the turn," while *edoi* corresponds to Latin *et hodie* (and today) in Iberian Romance. The refrain—"it's my turn . . . today it's my turn"—would thus be the heart around which the rest of the poem is built. The word *leli*, occurring six times in the last two strophes, is said by the two scholars to represent Arabic *laylī*, meaning "my night." Pedro Anes Solaz was attached to the court of King Alfonso X, and Toledo was still a bilingual city, making it odd but not entirely unthinkable that some Arabic would enter the text, just as (often bawdy) kharjas in Hebrew and Iberian Romance were sometimes incorporated into Arabic muwashshah. Cohen and Corriente further argue that the cantiga, in the final stanzas, portrays a rivalry between the narrator and another girl, both of whom evidently sleep with the same lover, but on alternate nights. In support of this claim, they cite another cantiga de amigo by Anes de Solaz that can also be interpreted as a scenario of rivalry between two women.

This fascinating interpretation involves a fair amount of creative deduction, and many unsettled questions remain. Why do Arabic phrases occur in this one cantiga and no other? Does the scene described belong to a harem, and, if so, what is it doing in the universe of the cantigas? But the gibberish theory is none too credible. My translation of the cantiga relies on the interpretation of Cohen and Corriente.

50 The penultimate line—missing from the cancioneiro because of a copyist's error—was proposed by the editor Manuel Rodrigues Lapa.

51 This might be a satire against soldiers reluctant to fight against the Moors. Chicken, a mild meat given to convalescents, was apparently considered the food of cowards. It's also possible that the troubadour was poking fun at some superstitious behavior of the king.

52 The ironic doubling of the possessive ("Thy my") reinforces the soldier's complaint: that the wages rightfully belonging to him are still in the hands of the king.

53 The cavalrymen who frightened the unidentified nobleman were the Zenata (or Zenete), a Berber tribe famed for horsemanship. They had come from North Africa to aid the Moors of Granada in their fight against the armies of Alfonso X. They rode on small saddle horses whose name—jennets—derived from that of the tribe.

54 As noted in the introduction, this cantiga is difficult to classify. It might be indirectly autobiographical, or narrated by a man afraid to face battle. The tone, in any case, is sympathetic.

56 The refrain literally states: "Between Ave and Eve / there's a great difference."

58 Berger corresponds to Vejer de la Frontera, a hilltop town not far from Cádiz. St. Anthony's fire was a popular name for erysipelas, a painful, bacteria-induced skin infection, as well as for ergotism, a disease caused by a fungus found in moldy rye and with symptoms ranging from convulsions to burning sores and eventual gangrene in the body's extremities. These diseases, conflated under the one name, spread in epidemic proportions during the Middle Ages. The ninety-first song of Alfonso X's *Cantigas de Santa Maria*

describes the devastating effects of St. Anthony's fire and the Virgin Mary's cure of it in France, where it killed thousands of people in the twelfth century. Monks from the French Order of Hospitallers of St. Anthony were dedicated to treating victims of the "fire."

59 Guarda is an ancient Portuguese town east and a little north of Coimbra. Instead of reading the word as a proper name, one can interpret *guarda* to mean a military guard, a protective force.

In the only cancioneiro containing this cantiga, it is the first of a group of songs attributed to King Alfonso X, but a note on the preceding page of the songbook seems to identify Sancho I (ruled Portugal from 1185 to 1211) as its author. Scholarly opinion weighs heavily in favor of crediting the cantiga to the Spanish king, even though he is not known to have written any other cantigas de amigo. King Sancho, on the other hand, is not known to have authored any other cantigas of whatever type.

60 The refrain may be literally rendered as "And oh God, will he come soon?" and the second line of the third stanza as "for whom I sigh."

65 Instead of a belfry, the original speaks of a churchyard.

67 It is unclear, from the two surviving copies of the cantiga, exactly how the refrain should end.

The chapel of St. Simón is on the island of the same name, in the Vigo estuary.

69 Here I've translated *ric'home*, a high-ranking nobleman, as "rich man," according to the etymological origin of the term. My rendering of the first line of the second stanza is conjectural; *ebenas*, at the end of that line in the original, is either a word of unknown meaning or a copyist's error.

72 This is the same Maria Perez lampooned by Pero da Ponte (in cantiga 17) and other troubadours. In the second stanza, what I've rendered as the "the evening dance" was probably more like a va-

riety show taking place at a royal or noble court. In that same stanza, the "something in hand" seems to be a double entendre, signifying both money and a man's sexual organ. The third, very deliberately ambiguous stanza literally reads: "Any man who wants to see Maria Perez on top [of the stage where she dances, or on top of himself in some sexual act] should take something [money and/or a ready penis] below."

73 Although set in the universe of the cantigas de amigo, this song is narrated by a man, making it technically a cantiga de amor. The uncertainty of the genre is reinforced by the conflicting references to the females: though collectively called "girls" (typical of cantigas de amigo), one of the three is the troubadour's "lady" (*senhor*).

74 In the dueling cantigas known as *tenções*, each troubadour gets equal time. This *tenção*, which survives in just one of the cancioneiros, is undoubtedly incomplete.

75 The missing rhyme in the fifth line of each stanza is called a *palavra perduda* in the poetic treatise found in the *Cancioneiro da Biblioteca Nacional* (or, in Occitan poetry, *rim estramp*). Sometimes, though not in this case, the nonrhyming line does rhyme with the corresponding line in successive stanzas.

77 Although not actually narrated by a female voice, the atmosphere and subject matter are decisively those of a cantiga de amigo.

80 The refrain literally reads: "but do you want to talk with me? / Let's talk about my friend."

82 The exact repetition of the end word, occurring here in the first and fourth lines of each stanza, was known as *dobre* among the Galician-Portuguese troubadours. In my translation, the repeated word sometimes takes a different form, in accord with the technique known as *mozdobre* (see the note to cantiga 16).

83 Although attributed to the troubadour Joam Lobeira in the only cancioneiro where it appears, this cantiga de amor is atypical, and some scholars have argued that it was a later addition to the older (and now vanished) songbook from which the surviving cancioneiro was copied. Other scholars, however, see this cantiga as proof that Lobeira was the author of *Amadis de Gaula*, a peninsular romance of chivalry that includes an amended version of the song, popularly known as the "Lay of Leonorette." The Spanish author of the oldest surviving edition of *Amadis*, printed in Zaragoza in 1508, acknowledged that it was based on an earlier, now lost version, and in the mid-fifteenth century a Portuguese chronicler attributed the authorship of *Amadis* to one Vasco de Lobeira, who was possibly Joam Lobeira's descendant.

84 The shrine might have been located in Vale de Prados, Northeast Portugal, or in Valdeprados, Spain (near Segovia). My translation puts the mothers "inside the chapel" and the dancing girls "in the open air," but the original doesn't specify exactly where the mothers lit candles or where their daughters danced.

85 This seems to be a remake of a cantiga de amigo by Joam Zorro ("Bailemos agora, por Deus, ai velidas"). While it's possible that both cantigas were adaptations of a preexisting, traditional song, Airas Nunes was prone to borrow from his fellow troubadours, and another of his cantigas (no. 87) directly quotes lines from a Joam Zorro cantiga. Borrowing and reworking—in so-called *cantigas de seguir* (songs that follow)—was a respected part of a good troubadour's art. According to the fragmentary treatise on Galician-Portuguese troubadour songs, this borrowing could involve using the same melody and meter, the same melody and rhyme, or the same words of a stanza to mean—if the troubadour was clever enough—something different. The cantiga de seguir could serve to parody someone else's cantiga, to improve on it, or merely to offer a technically achieved variation.

86 The monks who wore black habits (second stanza) were Benedictines. White habits were used by the Cistercians (third stanza),

an order founded by reformist Benedictines in 1098. Pilgrims began traveling to Santiago de Compostela, the supposed burial place of St. James, in the tenth century.

The sixth line of the second stanza, missing in the surviving cancioneiros, was proposed by Manuel Rodrigues Lapa.

87 All four stanzas cite lines from cantigas by other troubadours.

90 This cantiga uses enjambment between strophes (as does cantiga 89) and even between the final strophe and the concluding, two-line fiinda (envoi). It's a perfect example of a cantiga *atéuda atá fiinda*, or "tied up until the fiinda," since only then does the cantiga reach a point of resolution.

91 The flowers are probably fleurs-de-lis on the shield and banners of her beloved, but they could refer to her parting gift, and they may also be a kind of metaphor for their love.

92 Paio Gomes Charinho, in 1286, after serving for two years as the Almirante Mayor (Lord Admiral) of Castile, was relieved of his post by King Sancho IV. This cantiga de amigo seems to be an ironic response to his being dismissed.

The fiinda is missing in the cancioneiros, but it would necessarily have begun with the same words that lead off the second and third stanzas.

93 Estela corresponds to modern-day Estella, a town in Navarre, southwest of Pamplona.

100 Crecente is located near Santiago de Compostela. The Sar is a small river.

101 In two other cantigas Joam Airas satirizes the superstitious who believed crows were omens and useful for soothsaying. Here, of course, the crow is not a crow at all.

104 This cantiga de amigo, which is a kind of counterpoint to the preceding cantiga, is unusual for being narrated exclusively from the mother's point of view.

108 Clearly inspired by a Pero Meogo cantiga (no. 77), Dinis's song is a masterpiece of rhythmic sensibility and semantic complexity. The entire cantiga turns on the recurring word *alva*, which can mean "white, pure" but also "dawn, daybreak."

116 In the original, lines 3–4 of the third stanza simply repeat what was said in the middle of the previous two stanzas, to the effect: "The vexation you feel (because of my love) couldn't vex me more."

121 In the original, the girl is "reciting" songs in the first stanza and "singing" them in the second, and the same verbs are repeated in the third and fourth stanzas, respectively.

Eating vulture meat was thought to confer divinatory powers.

123 Elvas is a town in Portugal's Alentejo region. According to a note in the cancioneiros, Vidal was Jewish and composed this and another cantiga de amor for a Jewish lady named Dona.

A third, middle stanza is missing in the two cancioneiros where the cantiga was copied. Rip Cohen has argued that each stanza should consist of six longer lines with internal rhyme rather than twelve shorter lines.

124 This tenção has come down to us not only in two of the cancioneiros but also through two seventeenth-century folios.

ABOUT THE GALICIAN-PORTUGUESE TROUBADOURS

AFONSO ANES DO COTOM, from Galicia, seems to have descended from low-ranking nobles. In the 1240s he was based at the court of Prince Alfonso of Castile (the future King Alfonso X), where he wrote around twenty surviving cantigas, most of them satiric and a few of them pornographic. *Nos. 11–12.*

AFONSO MENDES DE BESTEIROS, born into Portugal's minor nobility, took the side of Sancho II in the civil war that ended with Sancho being usurped by his brother, Afonso III, in 1248. It was probably at that point that the troubadour moved to Spain, where he spent a few years at the courts of Castile. Fourteen of his cantigas survive. *No. 53.*

AFONSO SANCHES (ca. 1288–1328), the author of fifteen cantigas, was the oldest and the favorite among King Dinis's nine children born out of wedlock. The one legitimate son, Afonso IV, was so jealous that he rebelled against him and against the king. Afonso Sanches took refuge in Castile and subsequently invaded northern Portugal. Only through the persistent intervention of Isabel, the Queen Mother, were the half brothers finally reconciled. *No. 124.*

AIRAS NUNES, a cleric from Galicia, wrote at least fifteen well-turned cantigas, touching on a wide variety of themes. He served in the Castilian court of Sancho IV from 1284 to 1289 and collaborated before that, as a scribe and probably also as a poet, on Alfonso X's *Cantigas de Santa Maria. Nos. 85–88.*

ALFONSO X, KING OF CASTILE AND LEÓN (1221–84), oversaw the production of a vast body of historical and scientific prose in

Castilian Spanish but wrote his poetry in Galician-Portuguese. Besides his contributions to the secular troubadour tradition (cantigas de escárnio, mainly), Alfonso X, "the Learned," compiled the *Cantigas de Santa Maria*, a collection of 420 songs—some written by him—in praise of the Virgin Mary. *Nos. 54–59.*

DINIS, KING OF PORTUGAL (1261–1325), born in Lisbon, ascended to the throne at the age of seventeen and ruled for forty-six years. An energetic patron of national culture, he founded his country's first university in 1290, in Lisbon (it was later transferred to Coimbra), and was himself one of the most prolific and talented Galician-Portuguese troubadours. No fewer than 137 of his cantigas have been preserved in the cancioneiros. *Nos. 108–18.*

ESTEVAM COELHO, active in the first decades of the fourteenth century, belonged to one of the last generations of Portuguese troubadours. His two cantigas published here are the only ones that have survived. He was the grandson of the troubadour Joam Soares Coelho. *Nos. 121–22.*

FERNANDO ESQUIO, who descended from Galicians with landed property, composed his cantigas around the year 1300. The nine that have come down to us are divided among the three main genres: de amor, de amigo, and de escárnio. *Nos. 119–20.*

FERNÃO GARCIA ESGARAVUNHA, whose twenty known cantigas date from the middle of the thirteenth century, was a member of the Sousa clan, one of the most powerful in Portugal's aristocracy. His father, Garcia Mendes de Eixo (mentioned in the introduction), composed one of the oldest surviving cantigas. There is also a surviving cantiga by Fernão's brother, Gonçalo Garcia de Sousa. *No. 44.*

FERNÃO RODRIGUES DE CALHEIROS, a Portuguese knight and one of the earliest Galician-Portuguese troubadours, wrote at least thirty-two cantigas in the first decades of the thirteenth century. *Nos. 4–5.*

GIL PERES CONDE, born and bred in Portugal, immigrated at some point to Castile, where he was attached to the courts of Alfonso X and his successor, Sancho IV. Nearly all his eighteen known cantigas are satirical. *Nos. 50–52.*

GIL SANCHES (ca. 1202–36), a son of Portugal's King Sancho I and a renowned cleric, composed a single surviving cantiga, one of the oldest ones preserved in the cancioneiros. *No. 3.*

JOAM AIRAS DE SANTIAGO, as his name suggests, hailed from the capital of Galicia, but he resided at the Castilian courts of Alfonso X and Sancho I and the Portuguese court of King Dinis. An exceptionally talented and prolific troubadour, he produced a varied output of more than eighty cantigas in the last decades of the thirteenth century. *Nos. 95–102.*

JOAM BAVECA, the author of at least thirty cantigas, seems to have been a Galician. Active in the mid-thirteenth century, he was part of the literary entourage of both Fernando III and his successor, Alfonso X. *Nos. 75–76.*

JOAM GARCIA DE GUILHADE, a Portuguese knight, lived for a time at the court of Alfonso X and made his living as a troubadour, employing jongleurs to play and sing his cantigas, fifty-four of which survive. They are notable for breaking with convention and for their effective use of irony. The troubadour mentions his own name in a number of cantigas, usually to poke fun at himself. *Nos. 21–30.*

JOAM LOBEIRA, a Portuguese knight connected to the courts of King Afonso III (1248–79) and King Dinis (1279–1325), composed at least one cantiga de escárnio and half a dozen cantigas de amor, though the status and authorship of the one published in this selection is disputed. *No. 83.*

JOAM LOPES DE ULHOA, from Galicia, belonged to a military order, possibly the Knights Templar or Knights Hospitaller, and there are documents suggesting that he ended up living in Portugal. His eighteen cantigas date from the mid-thirteenth century. *No. 49.*

JOAM SOARES COELHO, a Portuguese nobleman born sometime before 1220, lived as a young man in Castile, where he was attached to the court of Prince Alfonso (the future Alfonso X) and fought in the war to conquer the Algarve, then under the Moors. By 1249 he was back in Portugal, serving for the next three decades as a counselor to King Afonso III. The cancioneiros have preserved more than fifty of his cantigas. He was the grandfather of Estevam Coelho, one of the last Galician-Portuguese troubadours. *No. 43.*

JOAM VASQUES DE TALAVEIRA, a Castilian troubadour active in the final decades of the thirteenth century, resided at the courts of Alfonso X and his successor, Sancho IV. Twenty of his cantigas are recorded in the cancioneiros. *Nos. 72 and 74.*

JOAM ZORRO, based in Lisbon, seems to have been a jongleur in the service of King Dinis. Ten of his eleven known compositions are cantigas de amigo. *Nos. 103–7.*

JUIÃO BOLSEIRO, a Galician jongleur, spent time at the court of Alfonso X in the third quarter of the thirteenth century. Most of his eighteen surviving songs are cantigas de amigo. *Nos. 45–47.*

LOPO, a Galician jongleur active in the second quarter of the thirteenth century, was much slandered in four cantigas by the troubadour Martim Soares, who claimed that he sang and played abominably. Eleven of Lopo's cantigas have survived. *No. 8.*

LOURENÇO worked as a jongleur in the service of the troubadour Joam Garcia de Guilhade and eventually tried his own hand at composing cantigas, eighteen of which are recorded in the cancioneiros. A number of indignant troubadours scorned his pretensions to their art, giving rise to various tençoes, or dialogued cantigas, in which Lourenço defends himself against charges of compositional mediocrity. *Nos. 73–74.*

MARTIM CODAX, a Galician jongleur from the second half of the thirteenth century, wrote a sequence of seven cantigas de amigo telling the story of a girl's first love. Numbers 1 through 5 and number 7 are of particular interest for being among the very few secular cantigas for which the music has survived. *Nos. 60–66.*

MARTIM MOXA, a cleric from Galicia and the author of twenty known cantigas, was attached to the court of Alfonso X in the 1270s and continued, it seems, to have been an active troubadour in succeeding decades. *No. 94.*

MARTIM SOARES emulated the comparatively sophisticated models of the Occitan poets and was considered the greatest Galician-Portuguese troubadour of his period, spanning from 1235 to 1260. Eschewing the cantiga de amigo, he composed only cantigas de amor and de escárnio, about forty of which have come down to us. He hailed from the Portuguese town of Ponte de Lima, in northern Portugal, but spent a number of years in the royal courts of Castile. *Nos. 9–10.*

MEENDINHO, whose only surviving cantiga is set on a tiny island in the estuary of Vigo, was presumably Galician, and the diminutive form (*inho*) of his name, along with the absence of any other name, suggest the humble origins of a jongleur. *No. 67.*

NUNO ANES CERZEO, a Galician troubadour of noble lineage, was active in the middle of the thirteenth century. His small output—eight known cantigas—is marked by considerable diversity and technical bravura. *No. 42.*

NUNO FERNANDES TORNEOL, from Galicia, probably began composing his twenty-two known cantigas in the Castilian court of

357

Fernando III (reigned 1217–52). His only surviving cantiga de escárnio suggests that he was a knight in the service of a nobleman from Castile. *Nos. 13–14.*

OSOIRO ANES, a Galician nobleman who lived from around 1160 to 1220, was one of the first known troubadours to compose songs in Galician-Portuguese, eight of which have survived, all of them cantigas de amor. *Nos. 1–2.*

PAIO GOMES CHARINHO, a Galician nobleman, participated in the capture of Seville (1248) from the Moors, after which he held increasingly important administrative posts in the Kingdom of Castile. With the ascension of Sancho IV to the throne (1284), he became Lord Admiral of the realm. Relieved from this post a couple of years later, he was subsequently appointed adelantado mayor (royal governor) of Galicia. Gomes Charinho was assassinated in 1295, during the violent struggle for succession after Sancho IV's death. The cancioneiros have preserved close to thirty of his cantigas. *Nos. 89–92.*

PAIO SOARES DE TAVEIRÓS, a Galician troubadour, composed more than a dozen cantigas in the first decades of the thirteenth century. *Nos. 6–7.*

PEDRO AMIGO DE SEVILHA, probably a Galician jongleur, was part of Alfonso X's entourage throughout most of the king's thirty-two-year-long reign. He composed at least thirty-six cantigas. *No. 80.*

PEDRO ANES SOLAZ, author of a handful of surviving cantigas composed in the mid-thirteenth century, was Galician, probably from a low-ranking noble family. *No. 48.*

PERO DA PONTE, a Galician squire and troubadour present in the courts of Castile between 1235 and 1275, wrote more than fifty cantigas, notable for their variety and originality. He had a penchant for satiric cantigas de escárnio, some of which refer to the events of his day, such as the defeat of the Moors in Valencia (1238) and Seville (1248). *Nos. 15–20.*

PERO GARCIA BURGALÊS, as his name indicates, came from the Castilian city of Burgos, but his prolific activity as a troubadour— fifty-three known cantigas, including some that are unabashedly satirical—took place at the court of Alfonso X and perhaps, as well, at the court of Portugal's Afonso III. *Nos. 33–39.*

PERO GARCIA DE AMBROA, a jongleur from the province of La Coruña in Galicia, composed his fifteen known cantigas in the circle of troubadours attached to the court of Alfonso X. His peers ridiculed him in their songs for his low social standing, for his sexual liaisons with female dancers of dubious repute, and for not fulfilling a vow to make a pilgrimage to Jerusalem. He was afraid of sea storms, they said, and for this reason had never sailed farther east than Montpellier. The jongleur finally got over his fear, journeyed to the Holy Land, and died there, probably in 1257 or 1258. *No. 40.*

PERO GOMES BARROSO was the nonmarital son of a Portuguese nobleman but managed to surpass his legitimate half brothers in social standing, influence, and material prosperity. He fought in the capture of Seville (1248) from the Moors and served as Alfonso X's intermediary to pacify rebellious nobles in Granada (1273). Around a dozen of his cantigas are recorded in the cancioneiros. *No. 68.*

PERO GONÇALVES DE PORTOCARREIRO, born into a noble family from northern Portugal, composed just four known cantigas, sometime during the final decades of the thirteenth century. *No. 93.*

PERO MAFALDO, a Portuguese nobleman, composed at least nine cantigas at the court of Alfonso X and perhaps at other Spanish courts before returning to Portugal, probably in the early 1260s. *No. 41.*

PERO MEOGO, a Galician and possibly a cleric, was one of the many troubadours active in the mid-thirteenth century. All nine of his known cantigas de amigo are graced by the presence of a mountain stag, which scholars understand as a symbol of male sexuality. *Nos. 77–79.*

PERO VIVIÃES seems to have been a nobleman from Galicia. He composed at least eight cantigas in the second half of the thirteenth century. *No. 84.*

ROI FERNANDES DE SANTIAGO, a clergyman from the capital of Galicia, composed twenty-five surviving cantigas. One of them suggests that he accompanied Fernando III's army when it conquered Seville from the Moors, and he no doubt spent time at the court of Alfonso X. By the year 1284 he seems to have retired to a monastery in Santiago. *Nos. 81–82.*

ROI PAIS DE RIBELA, a Galician and the author of at least twenty-one cantigas, consorted with the troubadours Pero Garcia Burgalês and Pero Garcia de Ambroa, no doubt at the court of King Alfonso X. *Nos. 69–71.*

ROI QUEIMADO belonged to Portugal's minor nobility. He probably composed the first of his twenty-four known cantigas in the 1240s, when he began frequenting the royal courts of Castile. *Nos. 31–32.*

VASCO MARTINS DE RESENDE, a Portuguese nobleman, was part of King Dinis's entourage in the second decade of the 1300s. He was among the last of the Galician-Portuguese troubadours and has only one surviving cantiga, though he apparently composed others. *No. 124.*

VIDAL, one of the last Galician-Portuguese troubadours, is identified in the cancioneiros as "the Jew from Elvas" (a Portuguese town close to the Spanish border, about 150 miles east of Lisbon). A note preceding his two recorded cantigas de amor, both of which are incomplete, makes a point of justifying the inclusion of a Jewish troubadour, saying that "it is good not to let the good things a man produces be lost." *No. 123.*

BIBLIOGRAPHY

Editions

The bibliography of my *113 Galician-Portuguese Troubadour Poems* listed a number of critical editions for individual troubadours—by the scholars Leodegário A. de Azevedo, Pierre Blasco, Celso Ferreira da Cunha, Jesús Montoya Martínez, Saverio Panunzio, Erilde Reali, José Luis Rodríguez, Luciana Stegagno Picchio, Valeria Bertolucci Pizzorusso, Giuseppe Tavani, Fernanda Toriello, and Carmelo Zilli. More recent editions, cited below, have built and often improved on the work of these and other scholars. Besides those more recent editions, this section lists some of the classical, older editions for the main cantiga genres as well as anthologies that were useful to me and are still useful to interested readers.

Alvar, Carlos, and Vicente Beltrán. *Antología de la poesía gallego-portuguesa*. Madrid: Alhambra, 1985.

Árias Freixedo, Xosé Bieito. *Antoloxía da lírica galego-portuguesa*. Vigo: Xerais, 2003.

Cohen, Rip. *500 cantigas d'amigo*. Porto: Campos das Letras, 2003. This critical edition has greatly advanced our understanding of the cantiga de amigo genre.

———. *The "Cantigas d'Amigo": An English Translation*. Baltimore: JScholarship / Johns Hopkins University Press, 2010. Online edition.

Ferreira, Manuel Pedro. *Cantus coronatus: Sete cantigas d'El-Rei Dom Dinis*. Kassel: Reichenberter, 2005.

———. *O som de Martin Codax*. Lisbon: UNISYS/INCM, 1986.

Ferreiro, Manuel, director. *Universo cantigas: Edición crítica da poesía medieval galego-portuguesa*. Coruña: Universidade da Coruña, 2018–. This online database offers transcriptions for numerous cantigas (it will eventually include them all) as well as an excellent glossary. Accessible at http://universo cantigas.gal.

Gonçalves, Elsa, and Maria Ana Ramos. *A lírica galego-portuguesa*. Lisbon: Comunicação, 1985.

Lapa, Manuel Rodrigues. *Cantigas d'escarnho e de mal dizer dos cancioneiros medievais galego-portugueses.* 2nd ed. Vigo: Galaxia, 1970.

Lopes, Graça Videira. *Cantigas de escárnio e maldizer dos trovadores e jograis galego-portugueses.* Lisbon: Estampa, 2002.

Lopes, Graça Videira, Pedro Manuel Ferreira, et al. *Cantigas medievais galego-portuguesas.* Lisbon: Instituto de Estudos Medievais, FCSH/NOVA, 2011–. This online database contains transcriptions and helpful notes for all the secular cantigas, a glossary, biographies of the troubadours, facsimile images of the original manuscripts, and musical recordings. Accessible at http://cantigas.fcsh.unl.pt.

Mettmann, Walter. *Cantigas de Santa Maria.* Rev. ed. 4 vols. Madrid: Castalia, 1986–89.

Nunes, José Joaquim. *Cantigas d'amigo dos trovadores galego-portugueses.* 3 vols. Coimbra: Imprensa da Universidade, 1926–28.

———. *Cantigas d'amor dos trovadores galego-portugueses.* Coimbra: Imprensa da Universidade, 1932.

Reckert, Stephen, and Helder Macedo. *Do cancioneiro de amigo.* Lisbon: Assírio & Alvim, 1976.

Vasconcelos, Carolina Michaëlis de. *Cancioneiro da Ajuda.* 2 vols. Halle (Saale): Max Niemeyer, 1904. Reprinted Lisbon: INCM, 1990.

Additional Sources for the Introduction and Notes

Alvar, Carlos. *Textos trovadorescos sobre España y Portugal.* Madrid, Cupsa, 1978.

Ballesteros Berreta, Antonio. *Alfonso X el Sabio.* Barcelona: Salvat, 1963.

Blackburn, Paul. *Proensa: An Anthology of Troubadour Poetry.* Edited by George Economou. Berkeley: University of California Press, 1978.

Cohen, Rip. "aaBBB: The Strophic Form of Fernan Rodriguez de Calheiros 7." *Revista galega de filoloxía,* 2016, 33–51.

———. "Colometry and Internal Rhyme in Vidal, Judeu d'Elvas." *Ars Metrica* 12 (2010). www.ars-metrica.eu.

Cohen, Rip, and Federico Corriente. "*Lelia doura* Revisited." *La Corónica: A Journal of Medieval Hispanic Languages, Literatures, and Cultures* 31, no. 1 (Fall 2002): 19–40.

Dronke, Peter. *The Medieval Lyric*. London: Hutchinson, 1968.

Ferreira, Manuel Pedro. "Jograis, contrafacta, formas musicais: Cultura urbana nas *Cantigas de Santa Maria*." *Alcanate: Revistas de estudios Alfonsíes* 8 (2012–13): 43–53.

―――. "The Medieval Fate of the *Cantigas de Santa Maria*: Iberian Politics Meets Song." *Journal of the American Musicological Society* 69, no. 2 (2016): 295–353.

Goff, Jacques Le. *Les intellectuels au moyen age*. Paris: Seuil, 1985.

Heur, Jean-Marie d'. *Troubadours d'oc et troubadours galiciens-portugais*. Paris: Fundação Calouste Gulbenkian, 1973.

Lapa, Manuel Rodrigues. *Lições de Literatura Portuguesa*. Coimbra: Coimbra Editora, 1952.

Marrou, Henri-Irénée. *Les troubadours*. Paris: Points, 1971.

Menéndez Pidal, Ramón. *Poesía juglaresca y juglares*. Madrid: Espasa-Calpe, 1983 (1st ed. 1942).

Oliveira, António Resende de. *O trobador galego-português e o seu mundo*. Lisbon: Diário de Notícias, 2001.

Pizzorusso, Valeria Bertolucci. "La supplica di Guiraut Riquier e la risposta di Alfonso X di Castiglia." *Studi mediolatini e volgari* 14 (Bologna, 1966): 9–135.

Riquer, Martín de. *Los trovadores: Historia literaria y textos*. Barcelona: Planeta, 1983.

Souto Cabo, José António. *Os cavaleiros que fizeram as cantigas: Aproximação às origens socioculturais da lírica galego-portuguesa*. Niterói: Editora UFF, 2012.

Tavani, Giuseppe. *Trovadores e jograis: Introdução à poesia medieval galego-portuguesa*. Lisbon: Caminho, 2002.

Zenith, Richard. *113 Galician-Portuguese Troubadour Poems*. Manchester: Carcanet, 1995.

THE LOCKERT LIBRARY OF POETRY IN TRANSLATION

George Seferis: Collected Poems, 1924–1955, translated, edited, and introduced by Edmund Keeley and Philip Sherrard

Collected Poems of Lucio Piccolo, translated and edited by Brian Swann and Ruth Feldman

C. P. Cavafy: Collected Poems, translated by Edmund Kelley and Philip Sherrard and edited by George Savidis

Benny Andersen: Selected Poems, translated by Alexander Taylor

Selected Poetry of Andrea Zanzotto, edited and translated by Ruth Feldman and Brian Swann

Poems of René Char, translated and annotated by Mary Ann Caws and Jonathan Griffin†

Selected Poems of Tudor Arghezi, translated by Michael Impey and Brian Swann

"The Survivor" and Other Poems, by Tadeusz Różewicz, translated and introduced by Magnus J. Krynski and Robert A. Maguire

"Harsh World" and Other Poems, by Angel González, translated by Donald D. Walsh

Ritsos in Parentheses, translated and introduced by Edmund Keeley

Salamander: Selected Poems of Robert Marteau, translated by Anne Winters

Angelos Sikelianos: Selected Poems, translated and introduced by Edmund Keeley and Philip Sherrard†

Dante's "Rime," translated by Patrick S. Diehl

Selected Later Poems of Marie Luise Kaschnitz, translated by Lisel Mueller

Osip Mandelstam's "Stone," translated and introduced by Robert Tracy†

The Dawn Is Always New: Selected Poetry of Rocco Scotellaro, translated by Ruth Feldman and Brian Swann

Sounds, Feelings, Thoughts: Seventy Poems by Wisława Szymborska, translated and introduced by Magnus J. Krynski and Robert A. Maguire

George Seferis: Collected Poems, 1924–1955, Expanded Edition [bilingual], translated, edited, and introduced by Edmund Keeley and Philip Sherrard

The Man I Pretend to Be: "The Colloquies" and Selected Poems of Guido Gozzano, translated and edited by Michael Palma, with an introductory essay by Eugenio Montale

D'Après Tout: Poems by Jean Follain, translated by Heather McHugh†

Songs of Something Else: Selected Poems of Gunnar Ekelöf, translated by Leonard Nathan and James Larson

The Little Treasury of One Hundred People, One Poem Each, compiled by Fujiwara No Sadaie and translated by Tom Galt†

The Ellipse: Selected Poems of Leonardo Sinisgalli, translated by W. S. Di Pietro†

The Difficult Days by Roberto Sosa, translated by Jim Lindsey

Hymns and Fragments by Friedrich Hölderin, translated and introduced by Richard Sieburth

The Silence Afterwards: Selected Poems of Rolf Jacobsen, translated and edited by Roger Greenwald†

Rilke: Between Roots, selected poems rendered from the German by Rika Lesser†

In the Storm of Roses: Selected Poems, by Ingeborg Bachmann, translated, edited, and introduced by Mark Anderson†

Birds and Other Relations: Selected Poetry of Dezső Tandori, translated by Bruce Berlind

Brocade River Poems: Selected Works of the Tang Dynasty Courtesan Xue Tao, translated and introduced by Jeanne Larsen

The True Subject: Selected Poems of Faiz Ahmed Faiz, translated by Naomi Lazard

My Name on the Wind: Selected Poems of Diego Valeri, translated by Michael Palma

Aeschylus: The Suppliants, translated by Peter Burian

C. P. Cavafy: Collected Poems, Revised Edition, translated and introduced by Edmund Keeley and Philip Sherrard, edited by George Savidis

Foamy Sky: The Major Poems of Miklós Radnóti, selected and translated by Zsuzsanna Ozsváth and Frederick Turner†

La Fontaine's Bawdy: Of Libertines, Louts, and Lechers, translated by Norman R. Shapiro†

A Child Is Not a Knife: Selected Poems of Göran Sonnevi, translated and edited by Rika Lesser

George Seferis: Collected Poems, Revised Edition [English only], translated, edited, and introduced by Edmund Keeley and Philip Sherrard

Selected Poems of Shmuel HaNagid, translated by Peter Cole

The Late Poems of Meng Chiao, translated by David Hinton

Leopardi: Selected Poems, translated and introduced by Eamon Grennan

Through Naked Branches: Selected Poems of Tarjei Vesaas, translated and edited by Roger Greenwald†

The Complete Odes and Satires of Horace, translated with introduction and notes by Sidney Alexander

Selected Poems of Solomon Ibn Gabirol, translated by Peter Cole

Puerilities: Erotic Epigrams of "The Greek Anthology," translated by Daryl Hine

Night Journey by María Negroni, translated by Anne Twitty

The Poetess Counts to 100 and Bows Out: Selected Poems by Ana Enriqueta Terán, translated by Marcel Smith

Nothing Is Lost: Selected Poems by Edvard Kocbek, translated by Michael Scammell and Veno Taufer, and introduced by Michael Scammell, with a foreword by Charles Simic

The Complete Elegies of Sextus Propertius, translated with introduction and notes by Vincent Katz

Knowing the East, by Paul Claudel, translated with introduction and notes by James Lawler

Enough to Say It's Far: Selected Poems of Pak Chaesam, translated by David R. McCann and Jiwon Shin

In Hora Mortis / Under the Iron of the Moon: Poems, by Thomas Bernhard, translated by James Reidel

The Greener Meadow: Selected Poems by Luciano Erba, translated by Peter Robinson

The Dream of the Poem: Hebrew Poetry from Muslim and Christian Spain, 950–1492, translated, edited, and introduced by Peter Cole

The Collected Lyric Poems of Luís de Camões, translated by Landeg White

C. P. Cavafy: Collected Poems, Bilingual Edition, translated by Edmund Keeley and Philip Sherrard, edited by George Savidis, with a new preface by Robert Pinsky

Poems Under Saturn: Poèmes saturniens, by Paul Verlaine, translated and with an introduction by Karl Kirchwey

Final Matters: Selected Poems, 2004–2010, by Szilárd Borbély, translated by Ottilie Mulzet

Selected Poems of Giovanni Pascoli, translated by Taije Silverman with Marina Della Putta Johnston

After Callimachus: Poems, by Stephanie Burt, with a foreword by Mark Payne

Dear Ms. Schubert: Poems by Ewa Lipska, translated by Robin Davidson and Ewa Elżbieta Nowakowska, with a foreword by Adam Zagajewski

The Translator of Desires, by Muhyiddin Ibn 'Arabi, translated by Michael Sells

Cantigas: Galician-Portuguese Troubadour Poems, translated by Richard Zenith

The Owl and the Nightingale: A New Verse Translation, translated by Simon Armitage

† Out of print